THE BIG PICTURE 2

THE BIG PICTURE 2

LOOKING AT THE
SPIRITUAL MESSAGE FROM MOVIES

J. John & Mark Stibbe

Copyright © 2003 J. John & Mark Stibbe

08 07 06 05 04 03   7 6 5 4 3 2 1

First published 2003 by Authentic Lifestyle, an imprint of
Authentic Media, 9 Holdom Avenue, Bletchley, Milton Keynes, Bucks,
MK1 1QR, UK
and
P.O. Box 1047, Waynesboro, GA 30830-2047, USA

The right of J. John & Mark Stibbe to be identified as the authors of
this work has been asserted by them in accordance with the Copyright,
Designs and Patents Act 1988.

All rights reserved. No part of this publication may be reproduced or
transmitted in any form or by any means, electronic or mechanical,
including photocopy, recording or any information storage and retrieval
system, without permission in writing from the publisher.

British Library Cataloguing in Publication Data
A catalogue record for this book is available from the British Library

ISBN 1-86024-441-6

Unless otherwise indicated, all scriptural quotations are from the New
Living Translation, © 1996. Used by permission of Tyndale House
Publishers, Inc., P.O. Box 80, Wheaton, Illinois 60189, USA. All rights
reserved.
or
HOLY BIBLE, NEW INTERNATIONAL VERSION
Copyright © 1973, 1978, 1984 by International Bible Society. Used by permission of Hodder & Stoughton, a member of Hodder Headline Ltd.
All rights reserved.

Cover design by David Lund
Printed in Great Britain by Bell and Bain Ltd., Glasgow

Contents

	Introduction	1
1	Overcoming the Darkness: *The Lord of the Rings: The Fellowship of the Ring* Mark Stibbe	7
2	Fulfilling Your Potential: *Simon Birch* J. John	24
3	There Can Be Miracles: *The Green Mile* Mark Stibbe	34
4	Searching for Love: *Bridget Jones's Diary* J. John	53
5	The Art of Listening: *What Women Want* Mark and Alie Stibbe	68
6	Choices and Consequences: *Unfaithful* J. John	92
7	Is My Future Fixed?: *Minority Report* Mark Stibbe	103
8	It's What You Are on the Inside: *Shrek* J. John	123
	Conclusion	134

INTRODUCTION

In the summer of 2001, we met for one of our monthly breakfasts to look at and plan the teaching programme for St Andrews Church Chorleywood where we are both members. During the course of our meal we were amazed to find that God had been saying exactly the same thing to both of us: 'teach a sermon series using the movies'.

No sooner were these words out than we were planning what each of these services would look like and which movies we would use. We decided to have the series over eight Sunday nights between January and March 2002. We agreed that each service should be 90 minutes in length and focus on one movie. We also agreed that we would have a good mix of worship songs, readings, drama, testimonies and prayer. The basic structure of each meeting was to be as follows:

Welcome and Introduction
Prayer
Trailer for the Movie
Songs
Address

Dance/Drama/Song
Testimony or Reading
Song
Appeal
Prayer Ministry
Blessing
Refreshments

As we approached January, we became increasingly excited about this series. We decided to have dim lighting in the foyer and worship area, and to have movie music playing on CD as people came in. There was a tremendous buzz of anticipation as hundreds of people started to sit down. On the first night, J. John gave a warm and humorous welcome and introduced the series. The trailer for the first movie was shown (off the DVD version, where the theatrical trailers are nearly always part of the bonus features) and then Belinda Patrick – our worship director here at St Andrews – led us in praise songs that were carefully chosen for the occasion. Then came the first talk, entitled 'Searching for the Father', based on the first *Lara Croft* movie. Each point was illustrated by clips from the film.

We followed the talk (which lasted about 30 minutes) with more singing, focusing on God the Father, and a reading of a great modern version of the Parable of the Prodigal Son by Philip Yancey. This was followed by Belinda Patrick singing a song from the Broadway version of *The Lion King* (all about Simba's grief over his father's death), with a montage of clips (professionally edited) from *Lara Croft*. J. John then gave an invitation before a final song. This was followed by prophetic words that had been received in a prayer meeting before the service had begun. I read these out on the first night and each night subsequently. The blessing was then given. The congregation then had the choice of going to the lounge area for coke and popcorn (a lot more popular than coffee and biscuits!) or they came to the front to receive prayer from our ministry team. A great deal of healing took place on that first night, especially in the area of people's father wounds. Several people became Christians. This was to be repeated throughout the series.

We would have to say that these meetings were the most powerful and the most fun we have ever done anywhere. Using movies is a great way of connecting with contemporary culture. Movies are like visual parables and they make great illustrations of the timeless truths of the Gospel. Over the eight weeks we looked at *Lara Croft, The Godfather (Parts I, II and III), Fargo, Titanic, The Matrix, Cast Away, Saving Private Ryan,* and *Billy Elliot.* You can read the polished versions of these talks in the first volume entitled *The Big Picture.*

This year (2003), we looked at *The Lord of the Rings: The Fellowship of the Ring, Simon Birch, The Green Mile, Bridget Jones's Diary, What Women Want, Unfaithful, Minority Report* and *Shrek.* These talks are written up for you in this present volume.

What did we learn about from these eight meetings in 2002? The first thing is that using movies helped Christians to bring God into their leisure time. In fact, it helped Christians to realise that we can hear God anywhere anytime.

Secondly, using the movies in teaching is a great way of communicating the truths of the Bible to a generation who know little about Christianity. This approach appeals to a post-modern generation where the primary organ of receptivity is the eye rather than the ear.

Thirdly, the emotional impact of movie clips helped soften people's hearts. Movies and music, along with other forms of the creative arts, have a way of communicating truth at an affective rather than a purely cognitive level.

Fourthly, we kept the focus on Jesus Christ rather than a movie star by prioritising worship. We were very blessed in having someone like Belinda Patrick to lead us into the presence of God through inspirational, contemporary music.

Fifthly, we decided to make space for prophecy (hearing what God is saying about the people in the meetings). We are a charismatic church and we believe that God speaks through prophecy, and that this is a powerful tool in showing those who are not Christians that God is real (see 1 Corinthians 14:24–25). However, rather than have a time when church members could give words out loud and spontaneously, we had our listening time before each service. Powerful words were given in these prayer meetings and we relayed these before the blessing at the end of each service. Space does not permit me to tell some of the amazing stories of how many people were impacted by the accuracy of these words.

There is a lot more we could say. We are so convinced of the potential of films in worship that we are doing another series at St Andrews in January of 2004. You can find the details on our web site, www.st-andrews.org.uk.

Movies are therefore a great way of getting people to think about life's ultimate questions. The two series we have done so far have been packed out. Literally thousands have come along and heard about God's values and principles for life.

We are committed to the view that God speaks to people through films. We hope and pray that the chapters in this book enable you to get in touch with God. May God help you to enjoy films and to hear the gentle whispers of his Holy Spirit as you do so.

Mark Stibbe and J. John

1

Overcoming the Darkness

THE LORD OF THE RINGS: THE FELLOWSHIP OF THE RING

Mark Stibbe

2001, New Line Cinema/Wingnut Films

Dir.: Peter Jackson

Starring:
Elijah Wood
Ian McKellen
Liv Tyler
Viggo Mortensen
Cate Blanchett
John Rhys-Davies
Sean Astin
Orlando Bloom
Christopher Lee
Hugo Weaving
Sean Bean, Ian Holm
Andy Serkis (as Gollum)

Classification: PG

Based on Part 1 of J.R.R. TolKein's trilogy, *The Lord of the Rings*

Someone once said that you can't tell a book by its movie. That is generally true, except in the case of Peter Jackson's film version of J.R.R. Tolkien's *The Lord of the Rings: The Fellowship of the Ring*. For those of us who were brought up on Tolkien's epic tale of the hobbit Frodo, Jackson's film does not in any way disappoint. It is simply a five star rendition of the most popular book written in the twentieth century. Sitting in the cinema with my family watching the awe-inspiring landscapes of New Zealand, the valiant and heroic goodness of the little people of the Shires, the spectacular special effects and the great acting from an all star cast, was – to be honest – one of life's great moments. This film has inspired my children to read like no other film has, and it has also generated a great deal of healthy debate about the reality of the spiritual war going on in our world between good and evil, between light and darkness.

And that really is the great theme of *The Lord of the Rings*, which is why I have given this chapter the title 'Overcoming the Darkness'. For those of you who are not familiar with it, the story of Tolkien's trilogy goes something like this.

The Lord of the Rings describes, in amazing depth and detail, a mythical world known as Middle Earth. This is a pagan world that has not yet been enlightened by the Good News about Jesus. So even though Tolkien himself was a committed Christian, *The Lord of the Rings* is not a Christian allegory like, say, C.S. Lewis' *The Lion, The Witch and The Wardrobe*. There are echoes of the Bible in *The Lord of the Rings*, but the story itself depicts a world before Christ.

Three thousand years before the story proper begins, a ring with supernatural power was fashioned by the dark lord Sauron. Using this ring, Sauron sought to rule the whole of Middle Earth. But he was defeated in battle and the ring was captured by Isildor. Instead of throwing the ring back into the fires of Mordor (the only place where it could be destroyed), Isildor kept the ring for himself. Isildor was then killed and the ring was lost for many centuries, until, that is, it was discovered by a hobbit known as Bilbo Baggins.

Bilbo keeps the ring secretly and through its power his life is prolonged. However, the spirit of the dark lord Sauron has started to stir again. Sauron knows that the ring has been found and seeks to be reunited with the ring so that his domination of Middle Earth will be complete. Bilbo knows that he must give up the ring and it therefore passes to a hobbit called Frodo Baggins, played superbly in the movie by Elijah Wood. The first book, *The Fellowship of the Ring*, is about Frodo's acceptance of the challenge to face the darkness spreading like a cloud over Middle Earth. His quest is to take the ring back to the very heart of Sauron's kingdom, to Mount Doom, where the fires of Mordor still burn. There he will be called upon to throw the ring into the flames so that Sauron's plans will be ended and peace restored to Middle Earth.

This brings me to the first clip from the movie that I find so powerful. The story has been unfolding for a while and Frodo is now well aware of his great responsibility. He is speaking with Galadriel, the Queen of Lorien (played by Cate Blanchett). Frodo has been struggling to stay on the side of the light. He knows that he must not give in to the darkness but Sauron's seductive power is so strong and the temptation to misuse the ring is great too. As he speaks with Galadriel he opens his heart.

Clip One

FRODO: I cannot do this alone.

GALADRIEL: You are a ring-bearer, Frodo. To bear a ring of power is to be alone. This task was appointed to you and if you do not find a way, no-one will.

FRODO: Then I know what I must do. It's just I'm afraid to do it.

Galadriel bends down towards Frodo.

GALADRIEL: Even the smallest person can change the course of the future.

Scene skips to the evil army of Lord Sauron preparing to advance, and then to Frodo and the fellowship leaving Loriel by boat.

Galadriel, dressed in white, is standing on the riverbank bathed in light. She raises her hand to bless Frodo and the fellowship.

GALADRIEL: Farewell Frodo Baggins. I give you the light of Earendil, our most beloved star. May it be a light for you in dark places when all other lights go out.

This is one of the most powerful scenes in the movie for me. I remember sitting next to my four children in the cinema –

Philip, Hannah, Jonathan and Sam. At the time they were all under thirteen years of age. When Galadriel stooped towards Frodo and said, 'Even the smallest person can change the course of the future,' I looked at my children. Even little people can make a big difference. I found it intensely moving.

But for little people to make a big difference in an evil world – a world where the forces of darkness are plainly at work and indeed increasing in power – those little people have to choose the light. They have to make a decision to stand against the darkness and to stand for the light.

According to the Bible we are, all of us, presented with this choice during our lifetime here on the earth. The Bible says that God is light, and that Jesus Christ his one and only Son is the Light of the World. To the little ones (as Jesus calls his followers), the Bible gives a vision of being 'lights to the world'. This is the destiny of all those who follow the Lord Jesus Christ: to be a people who change the course of the future from death to life by being God's light bearers.

To fulfil that destiny we must make a choice. In 1 John 1:5 (a letter in the New Testament), John the apostle declares, 'This is the message he has given us to announce to you: God is light and there is no darkness in him at all'. To become a people that overcome the darkness we must, like Frodo, choose the light. Even though the temptation to give in to the alluring power of darkness may be very great, we must choose in this life to be children of the light. Even though the odds may be stacked against the light bearers of this world, the Bible declares about Jesus that 'the light shines in the darkness but the darkness has not overcome it' (John 1:5). Indeed, the Bible as a whole reveals that the darkness will never overcome the light; that even though darkness may spread more and more over the earth, in the final analysis the light will conquer the darkness and the cosmos will be purified.

All the more important then to make right choices while we have time! We need to make a choice now. Our destiny flows out of our decision. Neutrality is impossible. As William James, the philosopher of religion, once said, 'When you have to make a choice and don't make it, that in itself is a choice'. C.S. Lewis once put it in these very challenging words: 'When the author walks onto the stage, the play is over. God is going to invade, all right; but what is the good of saying you are on his side then? ... It will be too late then to choose your side. That will not be the time for choosing: it will be the time when we discover which side we really have chosen, whether we realized it before or not. Now, today, this moment, is our chance to choose the right side.'

Once we have made the choice to be a person of the light, the key from that moment on is to resist the temptation to go back to the darkness from which God has rescued us. Resisting temptation is of course difficult. Temptation would not be a problem if it did not have such a pull upon our hearts. In fact, most of us are very weak when it comes to temptation. We don't fall into temptation. We jump into it. Consider the following conversation:

'Son,' ordered a father, 'don't swim in that canal.'
'OK, Dad,' he answered.
But he came home carrying a wet bathing suit that evening.
'Where have you been?' demanded the father.
'Swimming in the canal,' answered the boy.

'Didn't I tell you not to swim there?' asked the father.

'Yes, Sir,' answered the boy.

'Why did you?' he asked.

'Well, Dad,' he explained, 'I had my bathing suit with me and I couldn't resist the temptation.'

'Why did you take your bathing suit with you?' he questioned.

'So I'd be prepared to swim, in case I was tempted,' he replied.

Throughout the story of *The Fellowship of the Ring*, Frodo faces one temptation after another. Throughout his journey to Mount Doom, Frodo is tempted to use the power of the ring but he resists its power. In this respect, the hobbits are stronger than human beings.

In the next clip, Gandalf is talking to Elrond, King of the Elves. The scene is Rivendell, and Elrond is bemoaning the way in which this present darkness has come upon Middle Earth. If only human beings had resisted temptation in the beginning.

Clip Two

ELROND: Gandalf! The ring cannot stay here. This peril belongs to all Middle Earth. They must decide now how to end it. The time of the Elves is over; my people are leaving these shores. Who will you look to when we are gone? The Dwarfs? They hide in the mountains seeking riches; they care nothing for the troubles of others.

> GANDALF: It is in men that we must place our hope.
>
> ELROND: Men! Men are weak. The race of men is falling, the blood of Numenor is all but spent, its pride and dignity forgotten. It is because of men the ring survives. I was there Gandalf, I was there 3,000 years ago when Isildor took the ring. I was there the day the strength of men failed. I led Isildor into the heart of Mount Doom, where the ring was forged – the one place it could be destroyed.
>
> *Flashback to Mount Doom where Elrond is speaking to Isildor, who holds the ring.*
>
> ELROND: Cast it into the fire! Destroy it!
>
> ISILDOR: No!
>
> ELROND: Isildor!
>
> *Back to Gandalf and Elrond in the present.*
>
> ELROND: It should have ended that day, but evil was allowed to endure. Isildor kept the ring, the line of kings is broken. There is no strength left in the world of men.

If the darkness is to be overcome in our world, we must choose to stay in the light. This means being strong in the face of temptation. As we read in 1 John 2:

> [15]Stop loving this evil world and all that it offers you, for when you love the world, you show that you do not have the love of the Father in you. [16]For the world offers only the lust for physical pleasure, the lust for everything we see, and pride in our

possessions. These are not from the Father. They are from this evil world.

Those who follow Jesus Christ are called to resist the lust for pleasure, the lust for power and the lust for possessions. The ring in Tolkien's trilogy represents all these things – 'one ring to rule them all and one ring to bind them'. The darkness has a great power to entice and then to entrap people. Isildor refused to resist the enticing power of the ring and was entrapped by it. This is always the final destination of a consistent failure to resist temptation. What looks so alluring has the power eventually not only to bind people but to destroy them.

In the Australian bush country grows a little plant called the 'sundew'. It has a slender stem and tiny, round leaves fringed with hairs that glisten with bright drops of liquid as delicate as fine dew. Woe to the insect, however, that dares to dance on it. Although its attractive clusters of red, white and pink blossoms are harmless, the leaves are deadly. The shiny moisture on each leaf is sticky and will imprison any bug that touches it. As an insect struggles to free itself, the vibration causes the leaves to close tightly around it. This innocent-looking plant then feeds on its victim.

Overcoming the darkness depends not only on choosing the light. It also depends upon resisting the darkness. Beyond that it depends upon pulling together with others. It depends, in other words, on working in community not in isolation.

I wonder if you've ever watched wild geese in flight. It is fascinating to read what has been discovered about their flight pattern and their in-flight habits. Four come to mind.

Those in front rotate their leadership. When one lead goose gets tired, it changes places with one in the wing of the V-formation and another flies at the head.

By flying as they do, the members of the flock create an upward air current for one another. Each flap of the wings literally creates an uplift for the bird immediately following. One author states that by flying in a V-formation, the whole flock gets 71 per cent greater flying range than if each goose flew on its own.

When one goose gets sick or wounded, two fall out of formation with it and follow it down to help and protect it. They stay with the struggler until it's able to fly again.

The geese in the rear of the formation are the ones who do the honking; it's their way of announcing that they're following and that all is well.

One lesson stands out above all others: it is the natural instinct of geese to work together. Whether it's rotating, flapping, helping or simply honking, the flock is in it together . . . which enables them to accomplish what they set out to do.

The Lord of the Rings is a great celebration of the power of friendship and camaraderie. Frodo Baggins does not take the quest on by himself, though ultimately it is his own individual destiny to be the bearer of the ring. Around him eight others form into what is called the Fellowship of the Ring. These nine together pledge to work as one to defeat the dark lord Sauron's powers and to restore peace to the whole of Middle Earth.

One of the finest scenes in the movie is when the fellowship is formed at Rivendell. As the visitors to Rivendell start arguing about who can possibly take the ring to Mount Doom, Frodo rises to the challenge:

Clip Three

FRODO: I'll take it, I will take it. I will take the ring to Mordor, though I do not know the way.

GANDALF: (smiling affectionately at the hobbit) I will help you bear this burden Frodo Baggins, as long as it is yours to bear.

ARAGORN: If by my life or death I can protect you I will.

Aragorn walks over to Frodo.

ARAGORN: You have my sword.

LEGOLAS: And you have my bow.

Legolas walks over to join Frodo.

GIMLI: And my axe.

Gimli walks over to Frodo and the others.

BORROMIR: You carry the fate of us all little one. If this is indeed the will of the council then Gondor will see it done.

From behind a bush Sam appears and rushes to stand beside Frodo.

SAM: Mr Frodo's not going anywhere without me.

ELROND: No, indeed it is hardly possible to separate you even when he is summoned to a secret council and you are not.

Merry and Pippin appear from behind a column.

> MERRY: Wait we are coming too.
>   *They run to join Frodo.*
> MERRY: You'll have to send us home tied up in a sack to stop us.
> PIPPIN: Anyway you need people of intelligence on this sort of mission, quest, thing.
> MERRY: Well that rules you out, Pip.
> ELROND: Nine companions! So be it. You shall be the Fellowship of the Ring!
> PIPPIN: Great! Where are we going?

What a wonderful picture of teamwork!

When Jesus Christ brought the light of God into this dark world, he chose just twelve people to accompany him. Through this team of twelve disciples, Jesus has caused the light of his kingdom to permeate throughout the entire world. In doing this, community has been the key. This is why the church is so vital. Together, in community, we can combine into a fellowship of the light. As long as we keep the darkness at bay, together we can enjoy a fellowship that makes us strong. As we read in 1 John 1:7 'If we are living in the light of God's presence, just as Christ is, then we have fellowship with each other'.

So the lesson of *The Lord of the Rings* is: first, choose the light; second, resist the darkness; third, *pull together*! No one person has got it all together. But altogether we've got it.

But there is a fourth and final lesson, and this must never be forgotten. Overcoming the darkness requires that we give our all. In other words, it requires sacrifice. The eradication of evil in the end usually boils down to a few making supreme sacrifices on behalf of the many. It involves vicarious suffering. This was true in World War II of the Royal Air Force, about whom Winston Churchill said, 'Never has so much been owed by so many to so few'. A few brave men and women held the forces of darkness at bay, and at huge cost.

In the final scene I want to mention from *The Lord of the Rings* the fellowship is beginning to break up. Borromir has died trying to protect Merry and Pippin. Merry and Pippin have been captured by the Uruk-hai. Frodo now stands weeping, resolving to go ahead to Mount Doom without his friends.

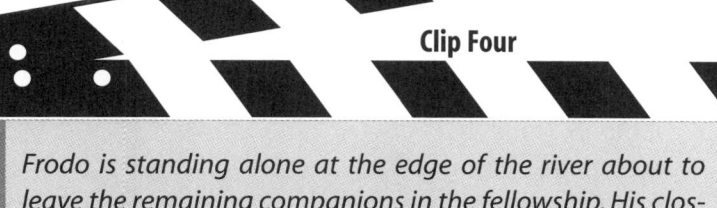

Clip Four

Frodo is standing alone at the edge of the river about to leave the remaining companions in the fellowship. His closest friend, Sam, is running through the woods calling out to him. Frodo is weeping and holding the ring in his opened hand.

Frodo says to himself: 'I wish the ring had never come to me. I wish none of this had happened.'

Frodo hears Gandalf's voice: 'So do all who live to see such times, but that is not for them to decide. All you have to decide is what you do with the time that is given to you.'

Frodo closes his hand over the ring and climbs in to a boat off the shore. We see Sam running through the trees to the river only to see Frodo rowing away.

> SAM: Frodo! No! Frodo!
> FRODO: (turns to his friend) No Sam.
> *Sam begins to run in to the water after Frodo.*
> FRODO: Go back Sam; I'm going to Mordor alone.
> SAM: Of course you are, and I'm coming with you.
> FRODO: You can't swim.
> *Sam begins to struggle and we see him go under the water.*
> FRODO: Sam!
> *The camera focuses on Sam drowning under the water. Just as it looks as if Sam is lost, Frodo's arm appears out of the light at the surface and grabs hold of Sam by the hand, pulling him out of the water into the boat.*
> SAM: I made a promise Mr Frodo: 'Don't you leave him, Sam Wise-Gangey.' And I don't mean to, I don't mean to.
> FRODO: Oh, Sam.
> *Frodo and Sam hug.*
> FRODO: Come on then.

A magazine once offered a prize for the best definition of a friend. Among the thousands of answers received were the following:

'One who multiplies joys, divides grief, and whose honesty is inviolable'

'One who understands our silence'

'A volume of sympathy bound in cloth'

'A watch that beats true for all time and never runs down'

The winning definition read:

'A friend is the one who comes in when the whole world has gone out'

Sam is that kind of friend – one who comes in when the whole world has gone out. He is a friend who is prepared to give his all, even to lay down his life for the one that he loves. Jeremy Taylor put it this way: 'By friendship you mean the greatest love, the greatest usefulness, the most open communication, the noblest sufferings, the severest truth, the heartiest counsel, and the greatest union of minds of which brave men and women are capable.'

In 1 John 3:16, the apostle John – a true friend to Jesus, known as the beloved disciple – speaks about the real meaning of love. He writes: 'We know what real love is because Christ gave up his life for us. And so we also ought to give up our lives for our Christian brothers and sisters.'

One of the abidingly attractive qualities of *The Lord of the Rings* is the extraordinarily Christ-like love of some of its noblest characters. In the scene above, Sam is prepared to lay down his life for his friend. Earlier in the film, at the Bridge of Khazad-Dum, Gandalf lays down his life for his friends. In that scene, Peter Jackson shows Gandalf falling backwards into the abyss, with his arms outstretched, in the perfect shape of a crucified man. This is in fact one of a number of places where the director gives an explicitly Christian resonance to scenes and dialogue that in Tolkien's original script are either barely visible or absent. Jackson has cleverly – and without ever being either crass or preachy – evoked some of the definitively Christian values of Tolkien's work. Nowhere is this more evident than in those scenes where sacrificial love is the dominant motif. Here true love, manifested supremely in the Calvary event, is poignantly and often beautifully represented. As the apostle John says: 'God showed how much he loved us by sending his only Son into the world so that we might have eternal life through him. This is real love. It is not that we loved God, but that he loved us and sent his Son as a sacrifice to take away our sins.' (1 John 4:9–10).

The movie version of *The Lord of the Rings: The Fellowship of the Ring* is a triumphant expression of what it means to overcome the darkness. The world in which we live is becoming increasingly beset by many evils. A dark cloud is spreading not only over the shires of Great Britain but over the whole globe. This cloud is made up of many things but behind it all lurks a sinister presence, a co-ordinating intelligence, a depraved and power-hungry personality, much like what we find in *The Lord of the Rings*. Who will combat this present darkness? Only those who choose the light, who resist the darkness, who pull together and who give their all.

Now of course the second of the three movies has hit the screens: *The Lord of the Rings: The Two Towers*. Who can have failed to spot the sinister connotations of the words 'the two towers'? Since the terrifying attack on the Twin Towers in Manhattan the world has grown less stable and secure. In the words of Tolkien (from *The Two Towers*), 'the world changes, and all that once was strong now proves unsure. How shall any tower withstand such numbers and such reckless hate?'

Tolkien's epic is truly a work for our times and for all times. It speaks to us powerfully and it stimulates hope that after all good will prevail. It is not a story, like some, that promotes an unhealthy interest in the occult. The quest of *The Lord of the*

Rings is to get rid of occult power (represented by the ring) not to use it. *The Lord of the Rings* is a book composed by a Christian with a very real and very clear moral compass. It is truly a bright light in our dark days.

In the final analysis, however, Tolkien's other writings (particularly his classic essay on fairy stories) suggest to me that he would not be content with us saying that his work contains fragments of light. For Tolkien, the true light was Jesus Christ, and the great story to which all stories ultimately point – at least in some measure – is the story of the Gospels. This story is not fiction but fact and guides us towards a vision of the world where there can truly be a happy ending.

Jesus Christ once said, 'I am the light of the world'. To alter the words of Galadriel ever so slightly, 'May he be a light for you in dark places, when all other lights go out'.

2

FULFILLING YOUR POTENTIAL

SIMON BIRCH

J. John

1998, Hollywood Pictures
Director: Mark Steven Johnson

Starring:
Joseph Mazzello
Ashley Judd
Jim Carrey
Ian Michael Smith

Classifiation: PG

Simon Birch is one of my favourite films; it really affected me and my family. Simple and heartfelt (without losing its touch on reality), it took me from laughter to tears and helped me to examine my own faith.

This is a truly inspirational story about a boy who was born with a growth disorder – Morquio Syndrome – which almost ended his life before it had begun. You must be warned: the film will leave a deep and lasting impression.

Directed by Mark Steven Johnson in 1998, *Simon Birch* is adapted from the novel *A Prayer for Owen Meany* by John Irving. It's a story that weaves love and friendship with faith and believing, focusing on one person's search for his past and another's quest for his purpose. The film is about faith in God and the ways that faith and love can enrich our lives. Tiny miracles take place all around us every day; and if we keep our eyes open to them, we surely can't fail to see that God exists. . . .

The opening scene takes place in a church graveyard, as a grown-up Joe Wenteworth (played by Jim Carrey) admits that Simon Birch is the reason he has ended up believing in God. The film then goes on to show just what happened to make Joe a believer.

Everything is framed as a flashback, as Joe revisits the scenes of his childhood in narration. 'I am doomed to remember a boy with a wrecked voice – not because of his voice or because he was the smallest person I ever knew, or even because he was the instrument of my mother's death, but because he is the reason I believe in God,' he recounts.

Simon, played by Ian Michael Smith (who actually suffers from Morquio Syndrome), is just over three feet tall. He was so tiny at birth that he was delivered with a sneeze rather than a contraction. No bigger than a baby bird, the doctors said he wouldn't last the night. But he did. Then they said he wouldn't last a week. But he did. . . .

Despite the fact that Simon is a miraculous baby, he soon becomes an outcast, even in his own home, as his parents are embittered by the misfortune they believe he has brought. They don't welcome him at birth, and they proceed to neglect him throughout his life.

An X-ray would have revealed a tiny heart, but in reality, Simon has an enormous heart. He is endowed, too, with a profound intellect. Throughout the story, Simon insists that 'God has made me the way I am for a reason,' and that 'God has a plan for everyone'.

This, despite the bad things that have happened to him, and to those around him. He is convinced that he's destined somehow to be an unlikely hero, an instrument of God for some purpose not yet revealed to him. And his belief is contagious.

When his best friend Joe (played by Joseph Mazzello) asks him how he can be so sure that God has made him different for a reason, he responds, 'I don't need proof. I have faith. The problem with you is you don't have faith. Faith is not in a floor plan.'

Such a firm faith in his destiny enables him to endure the indifference of his parents, the ridicule of other adults and the relentless teasing of children. Simon Birch is a rare and wonderful testament to the resilience of faith.

Joe and Simon originally gravitated towards each other because they were both social misfits – Simon because of his size, and Joe because his unmarried mother had always refused to reveal the identity of his father. Like Simon, Joe is the butt of jokes and scorn. But the boys develop a bond that allows them to deal with the ridicule they face.

Joe's mother (Ashley Judd) radiates virtue as Rebecca, a mother with enough love to treat the neglected Simon as a second son, despite being shunned by much of her conservative and judgemental community. Rebecca's big-hearted approach to life is one that we'd all do well to emulate. She makes sweaters for Simon when it's cold, she showers him with kind words, and makes him feel that he's as good as anyone in town.

Sadly, the fathomless faith of the 12-year-old Simon is in sharp contrast with the religious hypocrisy of the local church. Its humourless vicar, Revd Russell, sees Simon's intelligent questioning of 'church policy' as a threat. He's an inconsiderate and uptight minister who lacks the Christian values of tolerance, compassion and forgiveness. The truth is, Revd Russell envies this strange child's unshakeable faith.

Then there's the tyrannical Sunday School teacher, Miss Leavy (Jan Hooks), who is exasperated by the odd boy who believes he's an instrument of God. 'They don't belong here,' she says of his neglectful parents, 'and neither do you.' But Simon doesn't care what other people think; his own faith is the driving force.

The Bible states that 'without faith it is impossible to please God' (Hebrews 11:6). It also says that 'faith is the substance of things, hoped for, the evidence of things not seen' (Hebrews 11:1). This is the kind of amazing faith displayed by a victim of the Holocaust who had scratched a Star of David on the wall of a house in Germany. Beneath it was written this message:

> I believe in the sun – even when it does not shine.
> I believe in love – even when it is not shown.
> I believe in God – even when he does not speak.

The Greek word for faith means 'a firm conviction'. It believes what God says, because it is God who says it. We don't need a great faith; but we need faith in a great God, in Jesus Christ.

St Augustine once suggested that 'faith is to believe what you do not see; the reward of this faith is to see what you believe.' Several hundred years later, the rock star Bono, of U2, put it another way, in the song 'Walk On': 'I'm packing a suitcase for a place none of us has been – a place that has to be believed to be seen.'

Some things really do have to be believed to be seen. Faith is not like rubber, which weakens when it is stretched; it's like a muscle, which grows stronger with use. The Bible makes it clear that we must exercise our faith in order to stay firm within it.

It reminds me of a story. One day, a man was walking close to a steep cliff, when he lost his footing and slipped over the side. As he was falling, he was caught on a tree that was sticking out down the cliff. He found himself hanging from a branch with both hands. As he looked up, he saw he was a long way from the top. As he looked down, he saw he was a long way from the bottom.

At this point, the man decided that it was time to pray. He yelled out, 'God, if you're there, help me!' Immediately he heard a voice saying, 'I'm here my son, have no fear.' The man was startled at first by God's voice, but he pleaded, 'Can you help me?' God replied, 'Yes, I can, but you have to have faith. Do you trust me?' The man answered, 'Yes Lord, I trust you.' God said, 'Let go of the branch, trust me and everything will be alright.' The man looked down at the rocks below and then he looked up at the steep cliff above and yelled, 'Is anybody else up there?'

There are times when we have to take a step of faith, to let go and let God take over, even when the outcome is unknown. We can't live in doubt when we have prayed in faith. Let's not doubt our faith and believe our doubts. Faith grows when we put our belief into action: trust God for the unexpected, and let him surprise you by doing the unexplainable!

Faith, put simply, believes Jesus Christ. It's not just saying, 'I believe in Jesus Christ,' but 'I believe Jesus Christ.' True faith believes Jesus and then acts on it, so that we fulfil our potential as we allow God's Spirit to fill us and flow through us. Many of us are capable of greater things than we realise. When we do what we can, God will do what we can't.

Itzhak Perlman is one of the greatest classical musicians today. When he was four years old, two things happened to him, which shaped his future. First, he was crippled by polio; second, he heard a recording of the violinist Jascha Heifetz. Perlman said that although polio took away his legs, Heifetz's music gave him wings. It gave him a dream that set him on the road to musical greatness.

We are all, in different ways, faced with great opportunities disguised as impossible situations. If you cannot do great things, do small things in a great way!

Here's another story. A fire once destroyed a building that contained tons of ice. Although there were thousands of gallons of potentially fire-extinguishing water in there, the ice was no good as it was. The building was full of frozen assets.

It makes me wonder: are you experiencing all that God has for you? The Christian life is a marvellous adventure, an exciting journey. Many people – including Christians – seem frozen stiff. Do you want the abundant life and purpose that Jesus promised? How about fulfilling your potential? We should all aim higher. Don't set your sights too low!

You can become all that God created you to be – if you give yourself to Jesus, follow him wholeheartedly and allow the Holy Spirit to work in you and through you. Between tomorrow's dream and yesterday's regret comes today's opportunity. So let us become what we are capable of becoming! The real voyage of discovery consists not in seeking new landscapes, but in having new eyes. And remember, it's impossible to develop eyestrain from looking on the bright side of things.

> Two frogs fell into a deep cream bowl
> One was an optimistic soul
> But the other took the gloomy view
> 'I shall drown, I shall drown,' he cried
> And so will you.
>
> So with a last despairing cry
> He closed his eyes and said 'Goodbye.'
> But the other frog with a merry grin
> Said 'I can't get out, but I won't give in.
> I'll swim around till my strength is spent
> For having tried, I'll die content.'
>
> Bravely he swam, until it would seem
> His struggles began to churn the cream.
> On the top of the butter at last he stopped
> And out of the bowl he happily hopped.
> What is the moral, it's easily found
> If you can't get out, keep swimming around.

Clip One

It's a cold, snowy day, and Simon and Joe are chaperoning a group of children on a school bus. The driver, distracted for a moment by the excitable youngsters, turns back to see a deer in the road ahead of him. He swerves to avoid it, loses control and plunges the bus down through some trees and into a rushing river.

Although Joe tries to help the children, there is confusion and panic. Simon, sitting at the back of the bus, sees, in a moment of visionary clarity, what must be done. This is his moment. This is when he becomes a hero.

He stands on his seat and calls – with amazing authority – for attention. The bus falls silent, and Simon orders Joe to take one child at a time from the half-submerged vehicle to shore. He does so; but just when they think their work is done, Simon senses that someone is left behind. As the waters rise, he returns to find one last child trapped in his seat. Below the icy water, Simon frees his tangled foot, and the child escapes.

The bus suddenly lurches under the raging water as Joe swims back for Simon. But after an agonising wait, Simon comes to the surface, and Joe brings him to shore.

God wants us to be victors, not victims; to grow, not grovel; to soar, not sink; to overcome, not to be overwhelmed. It is a really good thing to see a film featuring a physically challenged child who is confident, full of faith and who ends up as the hero.

Simon Birch combines a heart-warming story with a great lesson on faith. Simon is like one of the people who are listed in Hebrews 11 as a 'hero', commended specifically for their faith. Simon becomes a hero of faith when he saves the children from the sinking bus.

No matter who we are, or what state we are in, if we have faith and put our trust in God, we can fulfil our potential. The good news is that the best season of our lives can be ahead of us, no matter what our age or circumstances – if we choose to make it.

Take Colonel Harland Sanders, for example. In 1952, at the age of 65, he decided to be adventurous with a chicken recipe of his own which he'd developed. Kentucky Fried Chicken, which was started with the funds from a social security cheque, is now one of the largest chains of restaurants in the world – more than a billion 'finger licking good' chicken dinners are served annually. Age is about mind over matter. If you don't mind, it really doesn't matter.

The winds of God are always blowing, but we must set the sails. 'Seek his will in all you do,' says the Bible, 'and he will direct your paths' (Proverbs 3:6). In Ephesians, we read that 'God is able to do far more than we would dare to ask or even dream of – infinitely beyond our highest prayers, desires, thoughts or hopes' (Ephesians 3:20). What an amazing, uplifting, inspirational statement. And you'd better believe it!

It's not always easy, of course. Even the disciples had to pray: 'Lord, increase our faith' (Luke 17:5). We'd do well to join them in that prayer. And we'd do well, too, to believe with all our heart that God will answer us.

General William Booth, founder of the Salvation Army, was once asked the secret of his remarkable life. Booth answered, 'I told the Lord Jesus, he could have all that there is of William Booth.' We can place our whole selves in the hands of God, in faith that he will use us to do wonderful things. No matter how broken or different our hearts, minds and bodies may be, God can turn us into the most unlikely of heroes.

And if you still don't believe me, just ask Simon Birch. . . .

3

THERE CAN BE MIRACLES

THE GREEN MILE
Mark Stibbe

1999, Castle Rock Entertainment/Darkwoods

Director: Frank Darabont

Starring:
Tom Hanks
David Morse
Michael Clarke Duncan

Classification: 18

Based on a story by Stephen King

The Green Mile is one of those films that takes you by surprise. Hearing that it is based on a Stephen King novel, you suspect that it is going to be a gruesome horror film. Although there are several scenes that are horrific (especially one unnecessarily graphic botched execution), the overall tale is actually extremely moving and indeed spiritual. Like *The Shawshank Redemption* – a film likewise directed by Frank Darabont, likewise filmed in a prison, and likewise based on a Stephen King story – *The Green Mile* is a really stirring story of how human and indeed divine goodness can arise in even the most desperate and bleak circumstances. *The Green Mile* is a film I keep revisiting and a novel I keep re-reading. It has become one of my top ten favourite movies.

So what's the story? *The Green Mile* refers to the green floor of death row in a 1930s Louisiana prison. It is both a stretch of floor leading to 'Old Sparky' (the electric chair) as well as a metaphor for the road that we must all take to our own deaths.

It is on this green mile that the action of most of the film takes place. The story revolves around a prison guard called Paul Edgecomb (played by Tom Hanks) who supervises the executions at the Cold Mountain Penitentiary during the years of the Great Depression. Even though Edgecomb does his job professionally, you also feel from his performance that it is something he does reluctantly. Maybe the Depression has forced him into this line of work. In any event, he performs his duties with humanity and compassion. Indeed, the power of this film lies not in great scenes of action but in the wonderfully realised relationships between Edgecomb and the prisoners on death row.

Onto death row comes an extraordinary prisoner, a giant of a black man called John Coffey (played by Michael Clarke Duncan). Coffey is a huge man with a childlike heart. He can barely spell. He is afraid of the dark. Yet he is a man who physically exudes great strength. Coffey is on the mile because he has been sentenced for the murder of two little girls. Later on in the film we learn that he is innocent of these charges. The immorality of racism and the questionable morality of capital punishment become major themes in the story as a result. But at the start of the film we don't know this and we are, like Edgecomb, drawn into the enigma of John Coffey.

Here is their first dialogue.

Clip One

The scene opens with Paul Edgecomb standing in front of John Coffey in a cell. Edgecomb's fellow prison warders are standing with him: Dean, 'Brutal' and Harry.

EDGECOMB: (referring to the handcuffs) If I let Harry take those off, you going to be nice?
Coffey nods his head in agreement.
Harry steps forward and unlocks the handcuffs.
EDGECOMB: Your name is John Coffey?
COFFEY: Yes sir, boss. Like the drink, only not spelt the same.
MARSHALL: Oh you can spell, can you?
COFFEY: Just my name boss.
EDGECOMB: My name is Paul Edgecomb. If I'm not here you can ask for these three gentlemen right there.
Camera pans to the three warders standing outside the cell.
EDGECOMB: Questions?
COFFEY: Do you leave the light on after bedtime? 'Cos I get a little scared in the dark sometimes. If it's a strange place.
EDGECOMB: It stays pretty bright around here all night long; we always keep a few lights burning out there in the corridor.
COFFEY: Corridor?

> EDGECOMB: Right out there.
> *Coffey turns and looks out from his cell then turns back and stretches out his hand to Edgecomb to shake it. The guards get nervous. Edgecomb pauses and then stretches out his arm and Edgecomb and Coffey shake hands.*
> *Edgecomb turns and leaves the cell.*
> EDGECOMB: You can sit.
> *Coffey turns and sits on the bed and the cell is locked.*
> *Camera focuses on Edgecomb's face through the bars and then on Coffey's face.*
> *Edgecomb looks surprised and perplexed by the new inmate on the Green Mile.*

From this point on the film focuses on Edgecomb's relationship first with several other condemned prisoners and then with Coffey himself. Of all the prisoners it is Coffey who becomes the focal character. As the plot unfolds it becomes clear that he is a really good man, a gentle giant, full of exceptional kindness. He is extremely sensitive to the beauty as well as the ugliness of humanity. Even the prison guards come to respect and even love John Coffey.

Not only that, Coffey is able to perform miracles. Edgecomb, suffering from an appalling bladder infection, is healed miraculously when Coffey lays his hands on him through the prison bars. A mouse called Mr Jingles – beloved by one of the other prisoners – is cruelly killed by one of the prison guards, Percy Whetmore, a loathsome individual. Coffey takes the mouse in his hands, breathes on the creature, and Mr Jingles is resuscita-ted supernaturally. Coffey is certainly no ordinary inmate. He is a man who performs miracles in the darkest place. As Edgecomb narrates in the trailer:

> Miracles are funny things. You never know when they're going to happen. And when they happen in a place like this, that's the most incredible miracle of all. This is the story of a miracle that happened where I work – on the Green Mile.

Later on in the film we learn that the governor of the prison, Hal Moore, is suffering emotional agony because his wife Melinda is dying of a brain tumour. Hal and Melinda are close friends of Edgecomb and his wife Jan. One night, lying in bed, Edgecomb conceives a plan to take Coffey to Melinda, even if it means risking going to prison himself. He figures that if Coffey can heal a bladder infection, maybe he can heal Melinda's tumour. If the plan is to succeed, however, Edgecomb must first persuade his colleagues on the green mile to help him. So he and his wife Jan invite them to a picnic lunch in their garden.

Clip Two

HARRY: You sure do know how to cook chicken.
JAN: Well, thank you.
DEAN: This is one delicious treat, ma'am.
JAN: Well I'm glad you are enjoying it.
DEAN: Hey Brutal, you going to hog all those potatoes?
BRUTAL: Yes I am.

EDGECOMB: (changing the subject, and referring to Jon Coffey bringing Mr jingles) You all saw what he did to the mouse.

BRUTAL: I could have gone the rest of the day without you bringing that up.

DEAN: I could have gone the rest of the year.

EDGECOMB: He did the same thing to me. He put his hands on me; he took my bladder infection away.

JAN: It's true, he came home that day and he was ... (pauses and smiles) ... all better.

DEAN: Oh now wait, you're talking about an authentic healing, a "Praise Jesus" miracle.

EDGECOMB: I am.

JAN: Oh yeah.

BRUTAL: Oh, well if you say it I accept it. What's it got to do with us?

JAN: (referring to the prison warder's wife) You're thinking about Melinda.

BRUTAL: Melinda? Melinda Moore?

JAN: Yes, oh Paul, do you really think you can help her?

EDGECOMB: Well, it's not a bladder infection or even a busted mouse. I think there might be a chance.

HARRY: Hold on there, you're talking about our jobs. Sneaking a sick woman in to a cellblock.

EDGECOMB: Oh no. Hal would never stand for that. You know him, he wouldn't believe anything even if it fell on him.

HARRY: So you're talking about taking John Coffey to her.

EDGECOMB: Yes.

HARRY: That's more than just our jobs, Paul. That's prison time if we get caught.

> DEAN: You're damn right it is.
> EDGECOMB: No, not for you, Dean. You see the way I figure it you stay back on the mile. That way you can deny everything ....
> BRUTAL: I'm sure she's a fine woman.
> JAN: The finest.
> EDGECOMB: What is happening to her is an offence, Brutal. To the eye, the ear and the heart.
> BRUTAL: I have no doubt, but we don't know her like you and Jan do, do we?
> HARRY: And let's not forget, John Coffey is a murderer. What if he escapes? I would hate to lose my job and go to prison, but I'd hate worse to have a dead child on my conscience.
> EDGECOMB: I don't think that's going happen. In fact I don't think he did it at all. I do not see God putting a gift like that in the hands of a man who would kill a child.
> HARRY: Well that's a very tender notion but the man is on death row for the crime and plus he's huge. If he tried to get away it would take a lot of bullets to stop him.
> BRUTAL: No, we'd all have shotguns and I'd issue the sidearms. I would insist on that. If he tried anything, anything at all we would have to take him down. You understand. So tell us what you had in mind.

It is truly remarkable to see such an open discussion of spiritual healing in a modern movie. 'You're talking about an authentic healing?' asks Dean. He qualifies this by adding, 'a "Praise Jesus" miracle'. Edgecomb readily confesses that he is, and Brutal (played with customary grace by David Morse) replies, 'well, if you say it, I accept it'. No further proof required!

In addition to identifying Coffey's extraordinary gift, Edgecomb expresses for the first time his belief that Coffey is totally innocent of the charges brought against him. 'I do not see God putting a gift like that in the hands of a man who would kill a child,' he says. Edgecomb has already done some research on Coffey outside the prison. He has visited the lawyer who defended him, who informs Edgecomb that no one knew where Coffey had come from. It was like he just 'dropped out of heaven'. Now, around the table in his own garden, Edgecomb finally confesses what his instincts have been telling him right from the start: Coffey is an innocent man about to die for another's sins.

Clip Three

So the story continues. The guards agree to help their boss, Paul Edgecomb. Dean stays behind to hold the fort while Edgecomb, Brutal and Harry take Coffey in a truck late at night to the house of Hal and Melinda Moore. Coffey goes to the front door, pushes past the perplexed and frightened Hal, and goes up the stairs to the bedroom where Melinda is lying. Her face is disfigured by suffering. The tumour has caused her mind to lose its clarity, and confusion and anger pour out of her mouth. John Coffey sits down on the bed next to Melinda as Hal and the others enter the room and watch. Even though Hal wants to intervene,

MELINDA: Why do you have so many scars? Who hurt you so badly?

COFFEY: I don't hardly remember, ma'am.

MELINDA: What's your name?

COFFEY: John Coffey ma'am, like the drink, only not spelt the same.

Coffey leans over Melinda.

COFFEY: Ma'am?

MELINDA: Yes, John Coffey.

COFFEY: (referring to her tumour) I see it

Melinda begins to cry.

MELINDA: What's happening?

COFFEY: Shhh, you be still now, you be so quiet and so still.

John Coffey leans right over her and inhales the illness from her. The house rocks. Lights brighten as Coffey takes Melinda's sickness into his own body.

As Coffey moves back away from Melinda we see her completely healed, her face is young and beautiful – no longer disfigured.

Hal sits on the bed and takes his wife by the hand.

MELINDA: How did I get here? We were going to the hospital remember?

HAL: Shh it doesn't matter. It doesn't matter anymore.

MELINDA: Did I have the X-ray? Did I?

EDGECOMB: Yes, yes, it was clear. There was no tumour.

Hal leans forward and embraces his wife, sobbing uncontrollably with relief at the miraculous transformation of his wife.

Notice the first thing Melinda says to Coffey here, 'Why do you have so many scars?' Perhaps at this point we should come clean about the very obvious parallels between John Coffey and Jesus Christ. John, like Jesus, drops out of heaven. John, like Jesus, is an innocent man full of purity. John, like Jesus, is a man of extraordinary love and compassion. John, like Jesus, is a man who is wrongly accused of a crime and executed for it. John, like Jesus, is a man who performs miracles, particularly miracles of healing. John, like Jesus, is a man of scars who takes into his own body the sicknesses and sins of others. John Coffey, in short, is one of the most powerful and obvious Christ figures in contemporary cinema. Indeed, you have to pinch yourself to remember that this is a Stephen King story!

In his introduction to the novel *The Green Mile*, Stephen King reveals that the parallels between John and Jesus are indeed intentional, and therefore not the imposition of an over-zealous Christian reading. Indeed, he informs us that even John Coffey's initials (JC) were created to bring about a greater alignment to the person of Jesus Christ. Originally John had been Luke Coffey. As King confesses, 'Luke Coffey became John Coffey (with a tip of the chapeau to William Faulkner, whose Christ-figure is Joe Christmas) . . . .'

Six hundred years before the birth of Jesus Christ, a prophet called Isaiah had a vision of the death of Jesus on the Cross. You can find this in Isaiah chapter 53:

> [2] There was nothing beautiful or majestic about his appearance, nothing to attract us to him. [3] He was despised and rejected – a man of sorrows, acquainted with bitterest grief. We turned our

backs on him and looked the other way when he went by. He was despised, and we did not care.

⁴ Yet it was our weaknesses he carried; it was our sorrows that weighed him down. And we thought his troubles were a punishment from God for his own sins! ⁵ But he was wounded and crushed for our sins. He was beaten that we might have peace. He was whipped, and we were healed! ⁶ All of us have strayed away like sheep. We have left God's paths to follow our own. Yet the LORD laid on him the guilt and sins of us all.

⁷ He was oppressed and treated harshly, yet he never said a word. He was led as a lamb to the slaughter. And as a sheep is silent before the shearers, he did not open his mouth. ⁸ From prison and trial they led him away to his death. But who among the people realized that he was dying for their sins – that he was suffering their punishment? ⁹ He had done no wrong, and he never deceived anyone. But he was buried like a criminal; he was put in a rich man's grave.

John Coffey, like Jesus, exhibits many of the characteristics of this Suffering Servant of the Lord. More than anything else, John Coffey is someone who dies a cruel and terrible death for the sins of others. He is truly led like a lamb to the slaughter with quiet resignation. From prison and trial he is led away to his death. What could be more poignant than that?

In the last scene I want to reference, Edgecomb comes with Brutal to Coffey in his prison cell a few days before Coffey's execution. Edgecomb is tormented by guilt and grief at the prospect of killing an innocent man and wants somehow to get out of the predicament. Indeed, some have likened Paul Edgecomb to Pilate in this respect. Whatever the truth of that, the scene that follows is full of spiritual and specifically Christian resonances:

Clip Four

COFFEY: Hello boss.
EDGECOMB: Hello John. I guess you know we are coming down to it now. Another couple of days.
Edgecomb walks into the cell, takes a chair and sits opposite Coffey.
EDGECOMB: Is there anything special you want to eat for dinner that night? We can rustle you up almost anything.
COFFEY: Meatloaf would be nice, mash potatoes, gravy, okra, maybe some of that fine corn bread your missus make. If she don't mind.
EDGECOMB: Well what about a preacher, someone to say a little prayer or whatever.
COFFEY: Don't want no preacher. You can say a prayer if you like.
EDGECOMB: Me? Suppose I could if it came to that.

EDGECOMB: John I have to ask you something very important now.

COFFEY: I know what you are going to say and you don't have to say it.

EDGECOMB: No I do, I do have to say it. John, tell me what you want me to do. Do you want me to take you out of here? Just let you run away? See how far you can get?

COFFEY: Why would you do such a foolish thing?

EDGECOMB: On the day of my judgement, when I stand before God and he asks me why did I kill one of his true miracles, what am I going to say? That it was my job ... my job?

COFFEY: You tell God the Father, it was a kindness you done.

Coffey places his hands over Edgecomb's hands.

COFFEY: I know you're hurting, I can feel it on you. But you ought not to quit on it now. I want it to be over and done with. I do. I'm tired boss, tired of being on the road, lonely as a sparrow in the rain, and I'm tired of never having me a buddy to be with me to tell me where we're going to, coming from and why. Mostly I'm tired of people being ugly to each other. I'm tired of all the pain I feel here in the world every day; there's too much of it, it's like pieces of glass in my head all the time. Can you understand?

EDGECOMB: Yes John, yes I can.

BRUTAL: Well, there must be something we can do for you, John? There must be something that you want?

Coffey thinks for a moment then smiles.

COFFEY: I ain't never seen me a flick show.

> *The scene shifts to a hall in which a black and white film is playing on an old projector system. Coffey is the only one besides Edgecomb watching the film. It is a movie of Fred Astaire and Ginger Rogers dancing to the song 'I'm In Heaven' – a tune that Coffey will sing to himself as he sits in the electric chair a few days later.*

As Edgecomb prepares Coffey for his last supper, the full angst of his predicament comes to the surface. Edgecomb simply cannot come to terms with the awful realisation that he is killing one of God's miracles. He offers Coffey a way out but Coffey will not let the cup pass. He stays the course. The execution scene that follows is one of the most harrowing in modern cinema. The room is laid out like a church, with chairs in rows facing not an altar but Old Sparky. The people who have come look like they are in their Sunday best clothes. As the execution is prepared even the guards weep. Edgecomb, who has had his hand shaken by Coffey at the start of the film, now steps forward to shake Coffey's hand at the end. John dies with extraordinary courage and dignity.

The Green Mile is a great story and a great film. It is also a film that invites a Christian interpretation. In Stephen King's novel, Coffey is very clearly portrayed as a Christian. His prayer goes as follows: 'Baby Jesus, meek and mild, pray for me, an orphan child. Be my strength, be my friend, be with me until the end.' In the novel, Paul Edgecomb is clearly depicted as a man with a Christian sensibility. After the death of one of his prisoners, Eduard Delacroix, he muses as follows:

> Only God could forgive sins, could and did, washing them away in the agonal blood of His crucified Son, but that did not change the responsibility of His children to atone for those sins (and even their simple errors of judgement) whenever possible. Atonement was powerful; it was the lock on the door you closed against the past.

The Green Mile, like other stories by King (such as *Desperation*, *The Stand*, *The Girl Who Loved Tom Gordon*, *Storm of the Century*, and *The Shawshank Redemption*) is a story filled with Christian themes. Indeed, in *The Green Mile*, the world's leading horror writer reveals that he is also one of our most spiritually attuned novelists. In this respect, King is very like his creation John Coffey, a person full of paradoxes!

In the final analysis, however, the power of *The Green Mile* lies in its portrayal of the miraculous. Miracles of healing have not been commonplace or seriously treated in twentieth century cinema, not least because of the anti-supernatural worldview of the Enlightenment period. But the days we are living in now are not Enlightenment but post-Enlightenment. This does not mean rejecting reason and science. It does however mean developing a more post-modern perspective in which the material and the spiritual can be integrated. As post-modernity progresses, films are becoming noticeably more serious about treating the spiritual dimensions of life, including the Christian dimension. Frank Darabont's faithful rendition of Stephen King's novel brings this dimension to the surface in a way that modern filmgoers can find accessible and non-preachy. It is a filmic answer to the great question posed by George Bernard Shaw's St Joan: 'Must a Christ die in every generation for those who have no imagination?'

I do not know what your perspective is on what Dean in *The Green Mile* calls 'Praise Jesus miracles'. All I can say is that since becoming a Christian I have seen many events that I regard as miraculous. I have seen clear evidence of the supernatural and life-giving power that flows into people's lives when we pray in the name of Jesus. Though I have seen some not healed, I have seen many who have. If you have a great need today, ask Jesus to reveal himself to you. Come to the one who died on the Cross that we might be saved, healed and delivered.

To encourage you I would like to end with the testimony of a person who wrote to me recently. She is a member of our church (St Andrews) and this is the story of what happened to her earlier this year (2003):

Dear Mark,
Firstly I want to thank you so much for St Andrews. If it weren't for St Andrews, I would still have a very despairing daughter, who came to the Alpha course almost two years ago and was changed into a happy, calm, contented and lovely human being, when life had treated her so badly. Through no fault of her own crcumstances, had made her bitter and helplessly lost. We are now very close and I feel St Andrews has introduced her to Jesus and he has given me back my loving daughter.

My daughter then encouraged me to go to Alpha, so I went to see what 'wonderful' thing had managed to change her so much. I too changed. Although always a believer, as J. John says in one of his videos, the Lord was in the boot of my car, safely locked away! Not any more! I went to the Beta Group after the Alpha course and became involved in sitting in on the next Alpha course. From then I have been involved in serving people who do not come to church through Lunch Break – a meeting for busy mums.

A lot has happened to me in the past fifteen months and I have met so many lovely Christian people. I myself was given the privilege of encouraging someone else to attend the Alpha course who was in a desperate state, and she has found God's love and is a changed person. That encouraged me so much, I can't tell you . . . .

Finally, when Marc Dupont came to do those healing meetings about eight weeks ago, I was helping with the team on Saturday, when Marc called anyone with digestive problems (I have a hiatus hernia) and several of us were prayed for.

On Wednesday evening I had a very strong feeling that I must go to Marc's last healing meeting. I got there late and someone kindly found me a seat as the church was bursting at the seams.

Within minutes Marc asked all the people with back problems to stand; I stood, having had a bad back since the age of 14 (not something that had come along with 'old age' as I am now 61!). Marc encouraged us to go to the front of the church to be prayed for. In my heart, I thought I couldn't be healed but I said to Jesus, 'if you need to give me more pain to be able to heal me, then please do it now'. He did – great pressure on the base of my spine and lots of movement inside.

Someone was praying over me from the front and back, it was a lovely feeling and very spiritual. I went home and heard a loud 'click' in my spine, but I was still in some pain as always!

I went to bed and in the night I was woken by another loud 'click' and a muscle movement in my spine. In the morning I stepped out of bed normally, not slowly, stiffly and painfully as usual . . . . I couldn't believe it . . . I still can't! It has improved daily, every day since (I've had 2 operations in the last 6 years!) My bonus is that now I can stretch my hamstrings (couldn't before). I can lie on my back or front in comfort. I can sit normally in a chair without being surrounded by cushions . . . . And much, much more.

An added bonus: when I visited my daughter in Australia, where she now lives, we actually went horse riding together – something I haven't been able to do since I was 14 years old. Although we rode bareback in the sea and my large horse sat down and dumped me in the water, it was brilliant, and I had no aches at all the next day even though on three occasions I jumped down from my steed as there was no one to help. I'm 5ft nothing and it was a very long way down! Did I lay the fleece?

Guess what? I had an Indian meal and my digestion is just fine!

I thank God every day for what he has done for my family and me. I even had the opportunity to speak at our ladies' club last week and instead of a talk I had prepared I felt very strongly that all this had been given to me so I had the opportunity to spread the word. I told them about my 'miracle'.

They asked me to close with a prayer and I, although very nervous, did that too.

I hope this letter encourages you.

4

SEARCHING FOR LOVE

BRIDGET JONES'S DIARY
J. John

2001, UIP

Director: Sharon Maguire

**Starring:
Renée Zellweger
Hugh Grant
Colin Firth**

Classification: 15

Bridget Jones's Diary is the film of the book of the newspaper column – a romantic comedy, documenting a year in the life of a single, thirty-something woman in London, played by Renée Zellweger.

It's the beginning of the New Year for Bridget Jones, who works at a London publishing house as a marketing assistant. Determined to improve her life by losing weight, cutting down on cigarettes and alcohol and finding Mr Right, Bridget begins a diary to record her uncensored thoughts.

She starts by making a list of 33 resolutions (of which, in the end, she manages to keep only one). Bridget has two main fixations: to create the right image for herself, and to find a responsible man who will be truly committed to her, instead of just using her and leaving.

Her affections are torn between her boss, the dangerous, exciting and attractive Daniel Cleaver (Hugh Grant) and the haughty, mysterious human-rights barrister, Mark Darcy (Colin Firth). The love triangle that follows draws loose parallels with Jane Austin's *Pride and Prejudice*.

Bridget Jones's Diary (together with its sequel *The Edge of Reason*) was written by Helen Fielding, and has sold over 10 million copies in 30 countries. It was an overwhelming and instant success, capturing the plight of the contemporary woman in a remarkably familiar and endearing light.

Many people saw flashes of themselves as they followed the delightfully dysfunctional Bridget through 'performance anxiety' at work, ever-failing diets and her insatiable longing for love. I smiled at the one-liners, laughed at the subtle and not-so-subtle comedy and nodded in sympathy with Bridget's all-too-familiar plight – and I'm male. Imagine the female reaction!

It was, perhaps, encouraging to find that you can be a domestic disaster, a social embarrassment, a professional no-hoper and a little overweight, and still have two handsome hunks fighting over you. . . . But beneath the humorous surface of the film lie glimpses of real sadness. This movie successfully combines comedy and truth, but the humour masks the real emotion.

Laughter can often be an antidote to the things that make us sad. The film communicates reality, however fictional. Whether we are single or married, we can relate, to some extent, to Bridget's frustrations. They prompt an examination of our own lives and relationships. It's a movie that makes us realise that what – or *who* – is on the inside is far more important than having the perfect body, the perfect career or saying all the right things at the right time.

It is completely natural that we – both women and men – want to fall in love and get married. After all, Bridget is living out the desire that God has planted in most people to find a life's partner. It was God (not a grumpy Adam) who declared, 'It is not right for the man to be alone.' Desire for companionship is quite a legitimate need, and God recognises this.

Bridget's desire to find a life partner who loves her is a virtue, not a flaw. It is the way she goes about it – leaving herself sexually open for exploitation – that is the problem.

The director of the movie, Sharon Maguire, suggests that 'primarily, this film is about loneliness, dressed up as a comic anecdote'. The theme is established from the very start, as Bridget is alone in her flat, drinking, depressed, wearing her penguin-patterned pyjamas, and listening to Jamie O'Neal's song 'All By Myself'. The film opens expressing this fear . . .

Clip One

Intense loneliness is at the root of all of Bridget's actions.

It's the end of a winter's evening. Bridget Jones is alone in her flat, wearing her penguin-patterned pyjamas. A fire is struggling to stay alight in the hearth, and *Frasier* is coming to an end on the TV. She has a glass of red wine in one hand, a cigarette and magazine in the

> other. Jamie O'Neal's song 'All By Myself' blasts from her stereo. Her magazine doubles as an air-guitar. She checks her answer-phone: 'You have no new messages', announces the electronic voice. She downs her wine, as the music soars:
>
> > When I was young, I never needed any one
> > And making love was just for fun ...
> > Those days are gone.
> > All by myself.
> > Don't wanna be all by myself, anymore.
>
> The drums crash in, Bridget smashes a pretend drum kit, kicks the air and sings into her rolled up magazine. 'Don't wanna be all by myself, anymore ...'

As Bridget records in her diary, 'Loneliness, far from being a rare and curious phenomenon, is the central and inevitable fact of human existence.' And she is not alone in thinking what she thinks. It was Emily Carr who observed, 'You come into the world alone and you go out of this world alone. Yet it seems to me that you are more alone while living than even going and coming.'

Mother Teresa observed that 'loneliness and the feeling of being unwanted is the most terrible poverty'. Even Albert Einstein once remarked, 'It is strange to be known so universally and yet be so lonely.'

Each of us feels lonely at times, and wants to be understood. We fill our time with events and pack meeting after meeting into our schedule, and phone call after e-mail. Yet, despite all the people that surround us and all the activity we engage in, we rarely connect deeply with others. We seem to have become a society of acquaintances, living vicarious 'friendships' instead through characters on the TV like those on the popular US sitcom *Friends*.

The rapid urbanisation of the world – a modern phenomenon that has spawned over 300 cities of more than one million people – has meant that people are packed closer together physically, yet live in greater isolation. London is like a thousand suburbs in search of a city. We are little islands of self-absorbed, self-contained individuals, cast adrift from the solid continent of community.

Society is characterised more by fear and suspicion than by friendship and neighbourliness. Loneliness assumes many forms, each equally undesirable – an unsatisfied inner ache, a vacuum, a craving for satisfaction. The human heart has an insatiable longing to be loved.

Loneliness is the feeling that you don't really matter to anyone, that you are not significant, that you are isolated. It can occur at any time in our lives, affecting the young and the elderly, the busy and the leisurely. A person can feel very lonely and yet be lost in a crowd; on the other hand, you can feel physically alone and yet have a strong sense of personal connection.

Research shows that the experiences which really trigger acute loneliness are the death of a life partner or other family member, a separation or divorce, a broken engagement and leaving your home for study or work. All these can prompt deep emotional trauma.

So it's not without reason that loneliness has been termed the most desolate word in the English language. The single person in particular lacks one of the most obvious antidotes to loneliness: a loving partner. It's made all the harder thanks to the unhelpful yet popular idea – or myth – that everyone should get married and live happily ever after. The implication is that if you're not married, you have somehow failed. Curiously, this myth still abounds, despite the fact that our culture also looks suspiciously on the institutions such as marriage.

Her friends are constantly telling Bridget Jones that she should find a man and settle down. Certainly, loneliness can lead to discouragement and even despair – yet the good news is that it doesn't have to. It can bring about, much more positively, greater insight, deeper understanding, a more realistic lifestyle and unselfish loving.

We can't always control our feelings, of course, but we can control the decisions and choices we make because of our feelings. Bridget is dissatisfied with herself, and even seems discontent with her own aims and values in life. Lurking beneath is a mass of insecurities. Every embarrassing moment serves to reinforce the critical view she holds of herself. This is a typical human tendency, one that we all seem to share.

Bridget believes that exercise and clean living is the key to her change, as many of us do. She changes her goals and the content of her bookshelf to adapt herself to a new set of rules. Her books fluctuate between 'What men want' and then 'How to get what you want'.

Clip Two

Bridget is turning over a new leaf. 'At times like this,' she records in her diary, 'continuing with one's life seems impossible, and eating the entire contents of one's fridge seems inevitable. I have two choices: to give up and accept permanent state of spinsterhood and eventually be eaten by Alsatians. Or not. And this time, I choose not. I will not be defeated.'

So, into the bin go the self-help books, which counsel what men want and how to get them. And onto the shelves, instead, go the new books about how to live without men. Cut to Bridget pedalling defiantly at the gym ... and falling off her bike. Cut to Bridget looking in the papers for jobs in TV. Cut to Bridget walking over a London bridge, head up, on a sunny day. She will not be defeated.

Many of us never seem satisfied. Jason Lehman once wrote:

> It was Spring, but it was Summer I wanted –
>   the warm days and the great outdoors.
>
> It was Summer, but it was Autumn I wanted –
>   the colourful leaves and the cool dry air.

It was Autumn, but it was Winter I wanted –
   the beautiful snow and the joy of the holiday season.

It was Winter, but it was Spring I wanted –
   the warmth and the blossoming of nature.

I was a child, but it was adulthood I wanted –
   the freedom and the respect.

I was 20, but it was 30 I wanted –
   to be mature and sophisticated.

I was middle-aged, but it was 20 I wanted –
   the youth and the free spirit.

I was retired, but it was middle-age I wanted –
   the presence of mind, without limitations.

Then my life was over, and I never got what I wanted.

We seek more pleasure, more treasure and more leisure. Today we idolise sex, wealth, fame, pleasure, power and physical beauty. 'How do I look?' has become the predominant question in life. We worship the profane trinity of Me, Myself and I.

Bridget kept account of her weight and calorie intake every day. Do we treat scales like an idol, bowing to see what they say about us, and letting their verdict determine how we feel?

The 23rd Psalm for Dieting

My diet is my shepherd, I shall be in want,
It makes me jog quietly round and round green pastures,
It leads me to quietly drink water,
And jump on and off the scales.
It guides me to resist all pleasurable food
For my figure's shape.
Even though I walk through the aisles of Sainsbury's
I will buy no Bovril
For you are with me;
Your measuring tape and your calorie counter
They confuse me.
You prepare a table before me
In the presence of the Tellytubbies.
You cover my lettuce with low-fat mayonnaise,
My diet coke overflows.
Surely a rumbling stomach and a feeling of irritability will be with me
All the days of my slimming plan
And I will worry about my weight forever.
(Dr Debbie Lovell)

Like Bridget, we strive to measure up, while wishing we could be known and loved for who we really are. It's a search, ultimately, for the unconditional love of God.

Clip Three

Bridget is leaving a dinner party early. Darcy has followed her out, stopping her on the stairs. The Christmas lights glow in the background; a taxi hoots outside the doors.

'I hear it didn't work out with Daniel Cleaver,' he says.
'No,' she replies.
'I'm delighted to hear it,' he adds.

At which point, Bridget spews words at Darcy. She feels like an idiot. She always feels like an idiot. She always puts her foot in it. She always says the wrong things. She always messes up. And people like Darcy know it.

Darcy says he's sorry for being so rude the first time they met at her mother's New Year's curry. In fact, he says he likes her. 'Despite appearances, I like you very much.'

And just as Bridget is spewing forth some more – 'Yes, apart from the drinking and smoking, the vulgar mother and the verbal diarrhoea ...' – he stuns her.

When Mark Darcy tells Bridget that he likes her just the way she is, he shows that he's the right choice because he's not asking her to compromise herself to meet his selfish needs. Instead, he's offering her unconditional love.

As a result, Bridget grows in self-respect, so that she is able to turn down the manipulative, self-centred Cleaver and finally turn to the man who quietly offers her respect and friendship, as well as romantic love.

The psychologist Freud wrote, 'People are hungry for love.' The psychologist Jung wrote, 'People are hungry for security.' The psychologist Adler wrote, 'People are hungry for significance.' *Bridget Jones's Diary* is about a woman who is hungry for all three – for love, security and significance.

We were all created with two major needs: fellowship with God and companionship with other human beings. There's no substitute for either. The spiritual and social instinct lies deep within every human being, and when this need remains unsatisfied, the seeds of loneliness can grow and flourish.

Jane Austen once wrote, 'Friendship is certainly the finest balm for the pangs of disappointed love.' Blaise Pascal believed that in every heart there exists a God-shaped vacuum. And centuries before him, Augustine wrote, 'God created man for himself and our hearts are restless until they find rest in him.' For this reason, the greatest need of every person is to seek an authentic relationship with God, the Great Physician, who has the remedy for every disorder of the human heart.

We are hungry for God and in him, ultimately, we find love, security and significance. Bridget, meanwhile, seeks a meaningful relationship to fill the space in her life, and she is restless and anxious. We need a relationship with God to fill the space, and then we need to place God at the centre of our relationships.

Like Bridget, we need to realise that we are never really alone. People may let us down. Friends may disappoint us. Families sometimes fracture. But God is looking out for us. God sees, God knows, God cares, God loves. And God forgives.

Clip Four

The snow outside is falling, Darcy is in Bridget's flat, and everything, finally, seems right with the world. She's next door in the bedroom, changing into some sexier underwear. Darcy, on his own, sees a book resting on the table. It's her diary. And it's open at the wrong page. 'Mark Darcy is rude. He's unpleasant. He's dull. No wonder his clever wife left him. I hate him! I hate him!'

'I see,' says Darcy, to himself. And at that, he walks out. Bridget hears a door slam shut. She looks out the window, and sees him trudging down the snowy street. She calls out, but he doesn't hear her, or won't hear her. Bridget runs into the dining room, and sees the open diary. Help. Immediately, it all makes sense.

Without stopping to get dressed (she simply flings a cardigan around her shoulders), she runs into the street. 'Mark!' she shouts. At which point, Mark emerges from a shop. The snow is still falling heavily. 'I'm so sorry,' she pleads. 'I didn't mean it. Well, I did, I suppose, but I didn't mean what I meant. Everyone knows diaries are so full of crap.'

'I know that,' replies Mark. 'I was just buying you a new one. Time to make a new start, perhaps.'

In Jane Austen's *Pride and Prejudice*, the hero's pride is levelled, the heroine's prejudice turns out to be unfounded and the two come together to live happily. Why not discard last year's diary and begin again with God?

Whether you are married, divorced, widowed or single, you are being proposed to. Jesus is proposing to you. God is always trying to give good things to us, but our hands are too full to receive them. So why not lay down our pain, pride, prejudice, preoccupations, possessions, and pursue Christ? Be assured: if you walk with him, look to him and expect help from him, he will never fail you.

How much does Jesus Christ love us? The apostle Paul, in his letter to the Ephesians, prayed that they would 'understand, as all God's people should, how wide, how long, how high and how deep is the love of Christ' (Ephesians 3:18). Wide, long, high and deep – that's four amazing ways in which Jesus' love grows for us.

Let's take them one at a time, starting with *wide*. Jesus' love is wide enough to include everybody who wants to receive it. The Bible tells us that 'God so loved the world . . . ' – but who does that include? Everybody. I take tremendous comfort in knowing that God's love for me is utterly realistic; and because he already knows the worst about me, no discovery can make him disillusioned about me, in the way I can become disillusioned about myself (and others).

There is nothing we can do to make God love us more. But the good news is that there's nothing we can do to make God love us less. He loves each one of us, as if we were the only one. One writer put it this way: 'If God had a fridge, your picture would be on it. If he had a wallet, your photo would be in it.

He sends you flowers every spring, and a sunrise every morning.'

Whenever you want to talk, he'll listen. He can live anywhere in the universe, and still he chose your heart. Because Jesus loves me, I don't have to prove my own self-worth.

Second, God's love is *long* enough to last forever. He says, 'I have loved you with an everlasting love' (Jeremiah 31:3). Psalm 81:2 says, 'God's love will last for all times'. That is so different to our kind of love. Human love wears out – that's why we have divorces. That's why we need God's love; for God's love never wears out. It is patient and persevering.

It's good news that God never gives up on us. He loves us on our good days and on our bad days, because God's love is not dependent on our response. God is love.

Third, God's love is *high* enough to be everywhere. The Bible says, 'neither height, nor depth will ever be able to separate us from the love of God which is in Christ Jesus.' There is no place we can go to hide from God's love – because it reaches the parts other loves can't reach. Being a Christian is all about being in a relationship with God – so we never have to be alone.

Fourth, God's love is *deep* enough to meet my needs. 'My only hope is your love. For my problems are too big for me to solve and are piled over my head,' writes the psalmist (Psalm 40:11–12). It's not hard to identify with that. No matter how big the problem, his love runs deeper.

Some people are in deep despair; some are in deep trouble. Some people are in deep distress; some are in deep loneliness. God's love is deeper still.

Where is God when you hit rock bottom? 'The eternal God,' says the Bible, 'is your refuge and underneath you are his everlasting arms.' God can catch us and support us if we will let him. Sometimes, God sends the brilliant light of a rainbow to remind us of his presence, lest we forget in our personal darkness his great and gracious promises to never leave us alone.

When we look at these four phrases – *height, depth, width* and *length* – we have the four dimensions of the Cross. We cannot talk about the love of God without talking of the Cross of Jesus Christ, because the ultimate demonstration of love is when someone gives their life for you. Jesus said, 'Greater love has no one than a person who lays down their life for their friends.' God demonstrated how much he loved us by dying for us.

Notice that he doesn't show his love by sending a romantic poem or dropping a bunch of red roses onto our doorstep. Instead, 'God showed his great love for us by sending Christ to die for us while we were still sinners.'

He shows he cares, not by a poem, but through cries of agony and excruciating pain. It's not champagne he drinks, but bitter wine. He doesn't bear roses in his arms, but a crown of thorns on his head. He doesn't bathe us in fine smelling perfume, but saves us through sweat and blood. God's proposal was nailed to the Cross. And he did it for us – that's true love.

I have found that many people – including Christians – find it easier to tell someone else that God loves them, than to say it to themselves. It probably has something to do with lingering feelings of guilt or inadequacy. But when you look at all that Jesus has said and done to show you how much you mean to him, such feelings will disappear. We may always sense the pangs of loneliness in our lives. But no matter, ultimately. For we all are of value to God.

5

THE ART OF LISTENING

WHAT WOMEN WANT

Mark and Alie Stibbe

> 2000, Icon Productions/Paramount Pictures
>
> Director: Nancy Meyers
>
> Starring:
> Mel Gibson
> Helen Hunt
> Marisa Tomei
> Alan Alder
>
> Classification: 12

Not long ago I typed 'what women want' into the search engine of my computer. The first site I hit contained this heartfelt quote from a middle-aged woman:

I've been reading about what women really want, according to prominent psychologists such as Sigmund Freud and the late Timothy Leary, since I was an undergraduate.... How presumptuous, I thought, for men to write about what women want.

As soon as I read this I realized what a fraud I was. Here I am, a man, writing a chapter on 'what women want'. What do I know? I have been married for twenty years, and I have a daughter, and of course I had a mother (not to mention a twin sister) but I am still wholly unqualified to answer this question.

To underline this a friend of mine the other day gave me a present, a paperback book entitled *Everything Men Understand About Women*, subtitled *The Mysteries Revealed*. On the top right corner, in a clever marketing ruse, the publishers had added the words, 'complete and exhaustive'. As I looked at the book I should have sensed something amiss, especially seeing that one of the authors was a Dr A. Ripov. But no, I fell for it. I opened the book to find that beyond the opening page the whole volume was completely devoid of any contents whatsoever. It was entirely blank from start to finish!

So, recognizing my great shortcomings in this area, I have enlisted the support of my wife, Alie, in the writing of this chapter. I know this does not therefore represent a wholly feminine perspective. But at least it is better than having the whole thing written by a man!

The answer to the question, 'what women want', forms the heart of the movie that we are looking at in the pages that follow. Sigmund Freud died with this question uppermost in his mind, and unanswered. It is a moot point of course whether women themselves know what they really want. One female writer hits the nail right on the head when she says:

> Women are complex creatures. They scream for equality, yet complain that chivalry is dead. They want financial independence, yet still expect the man to pay in restaurants. They complain about having to work twice as hard to attain

recognition and climb the career ladder, yet still want the freedom to stay at home and raise a family. They want social independence, yet give their men grief when they want to go off and do their own thing. It's no wonder that men are confused.

Women are indeed complex creatures, and yes, maybe they do have a hard time crystallising what they really want. But this did not prevent director Nancy Meyers being brave enough to address the issue in a bold, romantic comedy starring Mel Gibson and Helen Hunt.

What Women Want focuses, ironically, on a male character, Nick Marshall, played by Mel Gibson. Marshall was brought up in the 1950s by a troop of showgirls in Las Vegas. He was pampered by these scantily-clad ladies to such an extent that he grew up thinking that this was how all women were going to behave towards him. *What Women Want* is about his transformation from archetypal male chauvinist to sensitive friend when his electric hairdryer falls into his bath while his foot is in the water. He is given a near-fatal electric shock that renders him unconscious. When he comes round the next morning he realizes to his horror that he can hear everything women are thinking. Marshall can hear every piece of internal monologue going on inside a woman's head.

Thinking that he is going mad, Marshall visits Dr Perkins, a psychiatrist played with great verve and wit by Bet Midler. In the following scene, Marshall tries to persuade Perkins that he really does have the miraculous ability to hear what women are thinking:

Clip One

The scene opens with a hand banging on a black front door. Camera pans back and we see Nick Marshall is knocking. Marshall then rings persistently on the doorbell. We see the sign: 'Dr Perkins Marriage and Family Counselling'.

MARSHALL: Dr Perkins, you may not remember me. I'm Nick Marshall; I came here about 10 years ago with my ex-wife.

PERKINS: (says to herself) Oh, not him.

MARSHALL: Oh good, you remember me. I'm sorry to barge in on you like this but I don't know who to turn to.

They enter the house and sit in Dr Perkins' counselling room.

MARSHALL: I'm desperate. I'm afraid to go to work, I'm afraid of my doorwoman. I'm afraid to get a cup of coffee.

PERKINS: Mr Marshall, please slow down, slow down. Let me make sure I completely understand what it is you're saying.

MARSHALL: All right, all right. I hear what women think.

PERKINS: Yes... You know, Mr Marshall, this kind of imaginary displacement scenario really isn't my thing. I do however have a very good friend over at the university hospital who specializes in men with menopause, testosterone depletion, she's fabulous. I think what I'll do is just give her a ring and send you over there.

PERKINS: (says to herself) Why did I answer my door? I was so into buying that lamp on E-bay.

MARSHALL: How much was it going for?

PERKINS: How much was what going for?

MARSHALL: The lamp on E-bay.

PERKINS: (turning to see an E-Bay home page on her PC) Oh, I see. That's good. Very clever.

MARSHALL: All right, you don't believe me, well try another one. Go on, pick a number, give it a whirl, any number.

Marshall lies back on the couch.

PERKINS: OK. A number between one and a –

MARSHALL: A million. Why not?

PERKINS: One and a million.

Perkins shuts her eyes and thinks of a number.

MARSHALL: Six hundred and forty-four thousand, nine hundred and ninety-eight, ninety-nine . . . want to make a decision here?

Perkins utters an expletive then calms down.

PERKINS: OK, let's say I do believe you, that you can hear what women think, even though I'm a grown woman of . . . (Perkins says to herself '51') 47.

MARSHALL: Oh, my lips are sealed.

PERKINS: This is phenomenal!

Perkins grabs another chair and moves closer to Marshall.

> PERKINS: You can hear inside my head. Why would you want to get rid of such a brilliant gift? Mr Marshall, you know Freud died at the age of 83 still asking one question: 'What do women want?' Wouldn't it be strange and wonderful if you were the one man on earth finally able to answer that question? Listen to me Nick, something extraordinary and I think miraculous has happened to you. My advice is you must learn from this. You know, there isn't a single woman that I treat that doesn't wish her man understood her better. If men are from Mars and women are from Venus, then you speak Venutian. The world could be yours. I don't know how this happened to you or why, but you might just be the luckiest man on earth. Imagine the possibilities. If you know what women want – you can rule.
> *Marshall leans back on the psychiatrist's couch and smiles gleefully.*

'If men are from Mars and women from Venus, then you speak Venutian.' Bet Midler's character is here making reference to a best-selling book of the nineties, John Gray's *Men Are From Mars, Women Are From Venus*, subtitled, *A Practical Guide For Improving Your Communication and Getting What You Want in Your Relationships*. In that book John Gray was simply underlining something we have really known since the Garden of Eden: that men and women are different! 'Male and female God created them' (Genesis 1:27). God created men and women to be unique yet united. As we read in Genesis 2:

> [18] And the LORD God said, 'It is not good for the man to be alone. I will make a companion who will help him.'
> [22] Then the LORD God made a woman from the rib and brought her to Adam.
> [23] 'At last!' Adam exclaimed. 'She is part of my own flesh and bone! She will be called "woman," because she was taken out of a man.'

Someone has come up with nine reasons why God created Eve:

- God was worried that Adam would get lost in the garden and would not ask for directions
- God knew that one day Adam would need someone to help him find the remote control
- God knew Adam would never go out by himself and buy himself a new fig leaf
- God knew Adam would never make a doctor's or dentist's appointment on his own
- God knew Adam would never remember which night to put out the rubbish
- God knew Adam would never handle the responsibility of child birth
- God knew Adam would need help relocating his gardening implements
- God knew Adam would need someone else to blame
- God finished making Adam, scratched his head and said, 'I can do better than that!'

Actually, the real reason why God created Eve was for friendship. Woman was created as a companion or friend to man, and vice versa. God created men and women to complete each other not to compete with each other. The trouble came, however, when both Adam and Eve sought to live life on their own terms rather than God's. When they sinned in Eden they fell out with God and they fell out with each other. Instead of remaining in an equal friendship of love, intimacy and respect they degenerated into individualism. From that moment on the man sought identity and purpose in his work, the woman in her relationship to men (Genesis 3:16–19). In both cases, men and women began seeking meaning from the created rather than the Creator. Instead of looking to God for their security, self-worth and significance they started to look to their work, their achievements, their relationships, their possessions. This is the situation we still find ourselves in today.

Returning to our movie, Nick Marshall now has the gift of being able to hear what women think. He works for an advertising agency. The department he works for is now being run by a woman called Darcy McGuire. Marshall had thought that he was going to be running this department, but his boss had other ideas and hired Darcy instead. With his new found gift, Marshall starts to listen in on Darcy's thoughts as a way of undermining her work and getting ahead of the game, in the hope that she will be fired and he will get her job. In the following scene, Darcy has realised that her greatest achievement would be to get a commission from Nike women's division to put together a television advert for women's trainers. Marshall, who is beginning to like Darcy, listens in on Darcy's thoughts:

Clip Two

Marshall and Darcy are at work in the office, trying to come up with a new advertising slogan for Nike women's trainers.

DARCY: (thinks to herself, looking at Nick's drawing) Ah, this is good; more insightful than I would have thought. This line doesn't feel exactly right ...

MARSHALL: If you are thinking that, that line isn't perfect, I agree, it needs a little work.

DARCY: There is something not exactly right about it, isn't there? I mean, it's not bad, it's insightful actually; it's just, well . . . What do you think this woman is thinking?

MARSHALL: Well, err . . . let's see. She's thinking about what she wants out of life. What she's going to accomplish? How's she going to do all that? Women, you know they think about that a lot. I mean, surprisingly a lot. They worry all the time about everything.

DARCY: You're so right. How do you know that?

MARSHALL: Well ... you know, even I had a mother.

Darcy laughs.

DARCY: Well, maybe running is her time off from all of that? Maybe it gives her something she can't get any place else? Look at her! Gee I want to be her. She looks so free, doesn't she? No one's judging her;

there's no boss to worry about; no guys to worry about; no games to figure her way through.
MARSHALL: I like that – no games. That's good.
DARCY: That would be nice in life, wouldn't it? OK, can I just think for one second?
MARSHALL: Take your time.
DARCY: (thinks to herself) OK, no games, how do I get that in? She's running. It's early, it's quiet, just the sound of her feet on the asphalt. She likes to run alone; no pressure, no stress; this is the one place she can be herself. Look any way she wants, dress any way she wants, think any way she wants. No game playing, no rules. Games, sports, rules – playing by the rules, playing games versus playing ...

Marshall stands up and moves towards Darcy. Nodding his head as he listens to what she is saying to herself.

DARCY: Why are you nodding?
MARSHALL: Because I think you're on to something.
DARCY: Am I?
MARSHALL: Aren't you?
DARCY: I was thinking about a play on words. Something about games versus ... I feel like it goes on to something good, playing games versus playing ...
MARSHALL: Sport?
DARCY: Yes, thank you – do you like any of this?
MARSHALL: A lot. I like the idea you can be yourself on the road.
DARCY: I do too. Did I say that out loud? – Cos I was circling around the exact same thing. Which is great because we are both on the same ... sorry I'm not thinking straight, maybe my glands are swollen.

> MARSHALL: Well, maybe they should be more swollen – you're doing great. Nike – no games just ...
> DARCY: Sports! All right we should write that down.
> DARCY: (says to herself) Did he come up with that or did I?

An American newspaper recently asked a range of celebrities the question 'What do women want?' Sandra Bullock, Jodie Foster, Ashley Judd, Michelle Pfeiffer and Julia Louis-Dreyfus all came up with answers that can be boiled down to one word ... chocolate. Even Mel Gibson is quoted as saying, 'I think I've scratched the surface after 20 years of marriage. Women want chocolate and conversation.' Why?

> Chocolate is always there when you need it,
> Seven days a week, 52 weeks a year.
> It doesn't care if your hair's in a mess
> Or you're not wearing make-up and high heeled shoes
> Nor does it walk out if you're pregnant – it comforts you.
> Chocolate doesn't care how much you're paid,
> Or the level of your qualifications.
> Chocolate doesn't pass you over for promotion or pay rises.
> Chocolate doesn't snigger at your contribution in meetings,
> Or act irrationally if you ask for time off to care for a sick child.
> Chocolate doesn't misinterpret your actions if you touch it, or smile at it.
> Chocolate doesn't mentally undress you or push against you in the lift,

Or lay bets with its companions on the colour of your underwear.
Chocolate doesn't get impatient if the evening meal is late
Nor does it hit you if the meal is not to its liking or the baby cries.
Chocolate doesn't expect you to be awake and ready for love
When it gets home late smelling of smoke and alcohol.
Chocolate doesn't make unreasonable demands or play games
It accepts you as you are, without question,
And most importantly – it hugs you on the inside.

But chocolate and conversation are not what women really want; chocolate and conversation are superficial manifestations of much deeper needs. The need for conversation masks a desire to be heard, accepted, understood and affirmed. Woman want chocolate because it makes no unreasonable demands, because it doesn't play games.

I think we begin to see those deeper truths in the scene we have just looked at. Nick has been out and about listening to women. He has come up with an ad of a woman running that bears the caption *'Take the time'*. Darcy thinks he is on to something. She says she wants to be the woman in the picture. And *what* is the woman thinking. Nick says, 'She's thinking about all the things she wants to do and achieve, and how is she going to do that.' He says women worry all the time. Darcy is surprised at his perception. She takes some time to brainstorm the idea. Nick is happy to let her do this because, rather than wanting to understand her, he wants to steal her thoughts.

In Darcy's mind we see what turns out to be the formation of the final ad. She desperately wants to be the woman out running; free to be herself, not playing by the rules, no rules even, no games to play ... the road accepts you as you are.

Nick interrupts, and together they come up with *Nike: no games, just sport*. Darcy wonders who came up with that – her or him. Nick knows the answer; *she* did – but he's playing games. He's not playing by the rules. He's reading her thoughts and using them against her for his own advantage. Nick is deceiving her into thinking he understands, but he is manipulating her and using information to his own advantage. That is not what women want.

So what do women want? Alie's answer: to be heard, accepted, understood and affirmed. In the next scene we see how Nick's gift has begun to change him. He and Darcy have met for drinks in a restaurant. They begin to talk. Darcy is taken by the fact she has met someone who understands her and accepts her for who she is. Her thoughts and spoken words become almost indistinguishable. Too late, Nick realises he is falling in love with this woman and that his game playing has put him in an awkward situation of compromise.

Clip Three

Scene opens with Marshall and Darcy sitting in a bar with mellow jazz being played in the background.

DARCY: Here's to another great idea.
MARSHALL: What? Meeting for a drink?

DARCY: Yes, that's exactly what I wanted to say. Sometimes I think you're a bit of a mind reader.

MARSHALL: Oh, but I don't have to be a mind reader with you – because you always say what you think.

DARCY: I know, it's a bit of a curse.

MARSHALL: Are you kidding? It's a relief! An enormous relief! Do you know how rare that is? To actually say what you think.

DARCY: Do you have any idea how rare it is for someone to actually like that about me? Trust me, this has not been a great thing in my life. My ex-husband didn't love me, let's just put it that way.

MARSHALL: He didn't love you?

DARCY: (thinks to herself) Did I just say that?

DARCY: Oh God – err, I meant to say 'it', he didn't love 'it', but I spoke my mind. You want to know the truth? I'm not sure if he did really ever love me.

MARSHALL: Oh.

DARCY: Yes, there's a conversation starter. God, a smart person would just get so very drunk now.

MARSHALL: How long were you married?

DARCY: A little less than a year. I've been divorced about nine months now. We worked together. You know that, right?

MARSHALL: Oh yeah, I'd heard that. What was that like?

DARCY: It was ... great in the beginning, then it changed, became competitive. Suddenly the better I did the worse we did. The price I pay for being me. I know that now, no truly ... do you want to know all this about me?

MARSHALL: Keep going.

DARCY: Well, that's why I needed to get out there on my own, scary as it was. I mean not scary but ... well, yeah, I was kind of scared.
MARSHALL: Why?
DARCY: I don't know. Guess I wasn't sure I could do the job. I mean, I thought I could do it but I'm finding Sloan Curtis a much tougher place to navigate than I thought. (Pauses) I'm sorry, this is insensitive of me; I know your were up for my job. I'm sorry I'm the one who got it.
MARSHALL: No I'm not, I've learnt a lot from you.
DARCY: Like what?
MARSHALL: Like what! Well for starters you really love what you do.
DARCY: You really love what you do.
MARSHALL: No, not as much as you do.
DARCY: How can you say that? You're so great at it. You're so great at it, I think Dan's even wondering why he hired me. Really, I think the bloom is definitely off the rose. Do you want to hear something really great?
MARSHALL: Yeah
DARCY: I just closed on my first apartment ever; finally I own my own place.
Marshall smiles adoringly.
DARCY: What? Now I wish I was a mind reader.
MARSHALL: No, I was just thinking, how men like me can get so screwed up.
DARCY: I don't think there are men like you.
DARCY: (says to herself) If we kissed would it ruin everything?

> MARSHALL: Listen to me, I think you're one of the great women ...
> *She leans over and kisses him.*

This is a really beautiful scene and very artfully constructed by Nancy Meyers the director. In fact, the whole scene is shot in front of a set of mirrors and made to resemble a tableau or a painting. That aside, the really important thing about this scene is the way in which Darcy is now speaking. If you compare this scene with the previous one the differences are striking. In the previous one, Darcy was keeping her thoughts to herself and Nick had to use his gift to read her mind. In this scene Darcy says everything out loud – bar two statements. This shows how free she feels about being herself with Nick. Furthermore, the actual distribution of the dialogue is significant. She speaks 90 per cent of it, Nick Marshall only 10 per cent.

Now some might say this is because women speak more than men! Astronaut Michael Collins quoted the estimate that the average man speaks 25,000 words a day and the average woman 30,000. Then he added: 'Unfortunately, when I come home each day I've spoken my 25,000 and my wife hasn't started her 30,000.'

Whatever the case, Nick is now falling in love with Darcy, so he accepts her just as she is. More than that, he is absolutely attentive to every word she says; he is seeing eye-to-eye and ear-to-ear with her in this scene.

Now this is really important. The main thing a woman wants is to be accepted, valued and listened to! The last of these – listening – is really what this film is all about. Until Nick Marshall receives his miraculous gift, he simply doesn't listen to women at all. Once he receives his gift, he can hear everything that they are thinking. At first he is disturbed by this gift, but eventually he is transformed by it – to the extent that he really understands what women want. In fact, one of the most surprising and amusing scenes in the film is when Nick is lying on his bed watching women's TV and crying at the testimony of a woman who has lost weight and regained a sense of self-worth.

What has happened to this guy?!

He has discovered the art of listening – and not just ordinary listening. As Darcy says, 'You seem to know exactly what I'm thinking. Don't you know how rare that is?'

Stephen Covey published a best-selling book in the nineties, *The Seven Habits of Highly Effective People*. The fifth effective habit Covey calls 'empathic listening'. Effective people are empathic – they hear what other people are saying and feel what other people feel. Covey argues that we generally listen at four levels.

1. We ignore what's being said and make no effort to hear or understand.
2. We pretend to listen. We may nod from time to time or tune in when something interests us but generally we hear little.
3. We listen selectively, paying attention only to those things that we agree with or that support our positions and beliefs.
4. We listen attentively. We focus on the words and compare it to our own experiences, but pay little attention to the meaning.

To be effective people Covey argues that we have to move to a fifth level, 'empathic listening'. This means feeling what the person is expressing, not just understanding the intellectual content of the words.

Raquel Welch once said, 'You can't fake listening. It shows.'

One of our greatest problems in society today is the fact that men and women do not know how to communicate with each other effectively. They neither know how to articulate their feelings or hear another's viewpoint. Perhaps we need to hear the words of the Bible from James 1:19, 'My dear brothers and sisters, be quick to listen and slow to speak . . . ' Why? Because hearing is a faculty but listening is an art.

Nick Marshall learns how to listen and to listen *empathically*. This radically transforms his ability to relate to his work colleagues, his girlfriend and especially his daughter. In the final scene we've chosen, Nick has now lost his gift and finds himself in the ladies' toilets of a hotel where his daughter's high school is holding the Prom. His daughter has just been ditched by her game-playing, older boyfriend, Cameron.

Clip Four

The scene opens with Marshall bursting into the female toilets at his daughter Alex's Prom.

MARSHALL: Alex, you in here?
Sound of Alex crying in the background.
MARSHALL: Alex, it's me.
ALEX: What are you doing here?
MARSHALL: Oh, honey, you know I can't believe I screwed up. I wasn't there when you left for the Prom.
ALEX: Yeah, well that's not why I'm in here, so you can just go, OK?
MARSHALL: Oh boy, I feel awful. Are you OK? I mean, come on out, let me see how you look at least.
ALEX: I look like crap.
Marshall gets in to the toilet cubicle next to Alex and sits down.
MARSHALL: So what happened?
ALEX: If I told you you'd just freak out.
MARSHALL: What you got to lose? Try me.
ALEX : OK. Cameron and his friends, they had this big plan. They rented this hotel room, it was like a suite and basically I promised that I was going to ... I can't believe I'm going to say this to you – I promised him that I was going to sleep with him after the Prom. Then, like, an hour ago we were on the dance floor and I said, I'm sorry Cameron, I'm just not ready.

MARSHALL: Good! Good girl.
ALEX: Dad, come on.
MARSHALL: I'm sorry, I'm sorry. Go on.
ALEX: And I said, I'm sorry, and he cuts me off and then he says, 'I never should have asked a stupid sophomore to the Prom, what a waste.' And two seconds later he goes and meets up with his old girlfriend and starts making out with her. I mean, it's disgusting! A slut with a tongue ring. And then they were laughing, and I just can't go out there ever.

Marshall stands on the toilet seat in his cubicle and leans over and looks over the top of Alex's.

MARSHALL: Oh honey, I'm so proud of you.
ALEX: Dad! What are you doing?
MARSHALL: I'm sorry, but I am. Believe it or not I know what it's like to be a woman, and it's not as easy as it looks. But you stood up for yourself. Do you know how ahead of the game you were? Anyway a guy that treats you like that and talks to you like that, he's not worth it.
ALEX: Worth my time, yes I know.
MARSHALL: It's true; he's not.
ALEX: And he's a total game player and I hate that.

Marshall is brought up short by that last remark, recognising much of himself in that comment.

MARSHALL: You are so much smarter than me.

At this point Alex comes out of her cubicle and stands in the doorway facing her father.

MARSHALL: And look at you, that clown made out with a girl with a tongue ring over you? (Pauses) Honey, you look beautiful.
ALEX: Thanks. Take me home, Dad.

Alie writes: when Mark and I watched this movie together looking for significant clips, we hit on this one quickly. 'What do you see in this one?' Mark asked. Well, you can't live with a literary critic/film critic without taking on board a new way of looking at things . . . so I had a go. What struck me was the *setting* of this conversation. They are in the ladies' loos of a smart hotel. Nick has learned so much from his experience even the ladies' loos hold no fears for him. He rushes straight in!

He finds his daughter crying in a locked cubicle and sits in the next one to listen to what she is saying. And he is really listening now, because he knows how seriously he has messed up their father-daughter relationship.

What immediately struck me was the similarity of this setting to a confessional booth in a catholic church. The father or priest figure sits on one side and hears the confession of the anonymous person on the other. Nick's daughter has been up to this point an anonymous person; he doesn't really know her, and he hasn't really heard her. And what he has heard in her thoughts has shocked him.

Now his daughter begins to say out loud what has happened and what had been intended. Nick is so conscious of the wall between them that he tries to lever himself over it. But that is not the thing to do. He has to sit and hear her out; sit and listen.

Eventually she tells all and he realises he doesn't need his gift any more. She expects him to be cross, but Nick is very proud of what she has done.

The vital moment, the moment of denouement, is when she says, 'Cameron is such a game player'. Suddenly Nick realises he is as bad as the boyfriend he has criticised: he is such a game player too. He comes to his senses and says, 'You are so much further ahead in the game than I am'. She has dared to stand up for herself and be honest; he has been a low-life.

At this moment the roles are reversed and it is as if Nick becomes the penitent and his daughter is hearing his confession. The result of Nick's listening is that his daughter voluntarily comes out of the locked cubicle and walks around the wall that separates them to find him in a position of vulnerability and humility.

Notice all the symbolism here. Her words, 'Take me home, Dad,' are very important. She is now calling him Dad not Nick! And she now knows that he can offer her a place of understanding and security where she is not going to be criticised for who she is or the preferences she has. He now knows that ultimately he can trust her judgement. So it's a great moment, this scene between daughter and father in the toilets. Secure in the knowledge that Nick hears and accepts her, Alex dares to call him *father*. Though Nick still has to sort out his relationship with Darcy, this scene is in many ways the better finale.

At the start of this chapter we quoted a middle-aged woman on the internet saying:

> I've been reading about what women really want, according to prominent psychologists such as Sigmund Freud and the late Timothy Leary, since I was an undergraduate .... How presumptuous, I thought, for men to write about what women want.

What we didn't do was add her conclusion:

> So what is it that women want, if it is not a life focused on production and domination? What I want, as a woman, and as a human being, is the freedom to fully express and receive love ...

Or, as Alie put it earlier, to be heard, accepted, understood and affirmed. In the end, Marshall learns how to listen and, in the process, he learns how to love. As he undergoes this transformation, even his clothing changes – from black at the beginning to white at the end. All of us can make this journey of learning how to love and to be loved. All of us can make the journey from darkness to light.

The Bible tells the story of a woman who meets Jesus at a well on the edge of town. It is midday and the sun is beating down upon them both. Jesus, thirsty, asks for a drink. She, being a Samaritan, hesitates. Jews and Samaritans aren't supposed to speak to each other. But Jesus presses in. As he does so, he listens not only to what she is saying but also to what his Heavenly Father is saying about her. He offers her the living water of God's amazing grace. He also tells her (relying on prophetic insights into her character) that she has had five husbands and is now living with a man to whom she is not married. Having her soul exposed she recognises that she is in the presence of one who can hear her innermost thoughts. She wonders if he is the long-awaited Messiah and runs back into town to tell others. The whole population, pretty well, comes out to meet him, and by the end of the story both she and they are confessing Jesus as 'Saviour of the World'.

This incident, narrated in John's Gospel (chapter 4), highlights one great truth. There is a man who listens to both women and men, who knows our thoughts, and who offers us a way from darkness to light. His name is Jesus, the greatest listener who has ever lived. Through Jesus, we can dare to call God our Father and discover the acceptance that we have been searching for all our lives. All we have to do is acknowledge the sin that causes us to look to the created rather than the Creator. All we have to do is to receive God's free offer of forgiveness.

6

CHOICES AND CONSEQUENCES

UNFAITHFUL

J. John

> 2002, Twentieth Century Fox
>
> Director: Adrian Lyne
>
> Starring:
> Diane Lane
> Richard Gere
> Olivier Martinez
>
> Classification: 15

Unfaithful is directed by Adrian Lyne, and set in the suburbs of New York City. That's where Edward and Connie Sumner (played by Richard Gere and Diane Lane) live with their 9-year-old son, Charlie (Erik Per Sullivan).

Edward and Connie have been happily married for eleven years; they clearly love one another. Edward's career may be demanding, but it has provided a beautiful home and an affluent life for them, without losing the affection of his wife who, he believes, is the most wonderful part of every day. They both adore their son, Charlie.

Clip One

One very windy day, however, while Connie is out in the city, she struggles to keep her footing, and is blown straight into a dashing Frenchman who's carrying a pile of books. They land together in a heap on the floor.

This is Paul Martel (Olivier Martinez), a sickeningly good-looking 28-year-old who deals in rare books. After picking themselves up, and chasing around for his books and her shopping, Connie asks him to hail her a cab, which he tries – and fails – to do. She has badly grazed her knee in the fall, so he invites her up to his apartment to clean up the cut.

First she says no; but then, hesitating, and just as an empty cab passes, she accepts his invitation ...

Paul asks Connie to accept a gift, and directs her specifically along an aisle to the last book at the end of the second shelf from the top. He tells her which page to turn to, and then joins her in reciting the words: 'Be happy for this moment, for this moment is your life.' Has Paul planted this book for just such a moment as this? Feeling awkward and sensing trouble, Connie beats a hasty retreat home.

The next day, however, she decides to return to Paul's apartment, and phones him from a payphone at the train station. She wants to see him again and, even though she is painfully aware of how she could hurt her husband and son, she chooses to be unfaithful.

The phrase in the book – 'be happy for this moment, for this moment is your life' – really sets the tone for the rest of the film. Connie has chosen to live for the moment, yet her choice, whether she likes it or not, will define the rest of her life.

After her first adulterous encounter, she feels conflicting emotions of pleasure and regret. On the train home she seems tormented but, at the same time, she revels in what she's just experienced. Connie struggles with the choice that she made, yet decides that passion – and the fulfilment of desire – are worth the risk, even though she already has a happy relationship with her husband.

As soon as she decides to sleep with Paul, however, the lies begin, and Connie starts to lead a double life. Adultery isn't just about who you lie with; it's also about who you lie to. Anyone who builds a relationship on anything less than openness and honesty is building on shifting sand. There are moments in our lives that change everything.

This film shows powerfully how adultery can be irrational, and can cause irretrievable damage to those involved. It explores the hurt and devastation that everyone goes through. Connie is not in love with Paul – she knows nothing about him, in fact, and their relationship is based simply on lust. Paul is naïve, too, because he believes there'll be no price to pay if his actions are discovered.

Connie's passion, once unbridled, becomes almost like an obsession; it's a compulsive urge which begins to consume her. Her desire overrides the guilt she initially feels. The passion is like a drug and her highs come from pushing the affair to the very point of discovery.

Unfaithful is about one decision which affects the rest of Connie's life, and the people connected to her. Take her son, for example: in one instance, Connie fails to pick him up from school on time; in another, he gets out of bed to find her crying and is left confused as to why this is. Gradually, he becomes aware of the growing separation between his parents. His anxiety is revealed through small, poignant details, like wetting the bed.

Edward senses that he's losing his wife's affections, and when he discovers that Connie is not at the hair appointment she's meant to have arranged, he smells a rat. As if her lies and deception weren't enough, he, too, quickly falls into a downward spiral of suspicion and secrecy. He hires a private investigator who discovers the truth about Connie's affair. In the end, Edward confronts his wife's lover, and in a momentary fit of despair, accidentally kills him. Desperately, he tries to cover up his actions.

He disposes of the body but, as the police investigate, Connie gradually guesses that he's the murderer. The consequences will reverberate forever. In the end, then, Edward and Paul also become victims of a poor choice. The film clearly shows that our negative actions do have irreversible and damaging effects. In fact, this movie is very sobering. It's a powerful parable about the corrosive effects of adultery.

No matter how many horror stories we might hear, many of us still choose to get embroiled in relationships that we know will end in tears. Most of us have made choices that are wrong. And many people have experienced the subsequent pain in the breakdown of relationships, as a direct result of those choices. Of all the behaviour that can attack a marriage, adultery is clearly the most serious.

Adultery seems to promise pleasure, love and fulfilment, but in the end there is only shame, deceit, betrayal, ugliness and hurt. Adulterous love appears to be free; but it comes with a painfully high price. It shatters trust and severs friendship.

Marriage is about giving, but adultery is about taking. It denies love, degrades people, destroys families, defiles marriage and defies God. That's why God gave us the seventh commandment, which says, quite simply, 'Do not commit adultery' (Exodus 20:14).

God says 'No' to adultery because it attacks marriage. Jesus held marriage in high regard – 'a man leaves his father and mother and is joined to his wife,' he said, 'and the two are united into one. Since they are no longer two but one, let no one separate them, for God has joined them together' (Matthew 19:5–6).

Adultery breaks the unity of two people in marriage. Sex, after all, is a total giving of oneself, so we can't make love to one person and then expect no consequences if we choose to sleep with someone else. Many people end up feeling trapped by guilt, which they think might even be God's way of punishing them. But they're wrong. We bring it on ourselves.

Some people deal with guilt by denying it, others try to drown it with alcohol or drugs. Still others try deflecting it; they blame other people for their failures and faults. But we cannot escape the consequences of our own guilt.

'No amount of soap can make you clean,' said the prophet Jeremiah. 'You are stained with guilt.' Guilt is the corrosion of the soul. But how can we get rid of it? Ultimately, we can't deny it, drown it or deflect it. We can only dissolve it in the blood of Jesus Christ. Mercifully, hope abounds, because adultery is sin and Jesus Christ came to rescue sinners.

John's Gospel tells how a crowd brought an adulterous woman to Jesus. "'Teacher, this woman was caught in the very act of adultery. The law of Moses says to stone her. What do you say?" "All right, stone her," replied Jesus. "But let those who have never sinned throw the first stone." When the accusers heard this, they slipped away one by one. Jesus said to her, "Where are your accusers? Didn't even one of them condemn you?" "No Lord," she said. And Jesus said, "Neither do I. Go and sin no more."' (John 8:4–11). Jesus forgave the woman, but expected her to learn and not do it again.

In fact, Jesus was the only person who could have thrown a stone, being 'without sin'; but he didn't. Instead, he forgave her. We have seventeen different instances recorded in the Bible in which Jesus forgave a person and showed mercy.

If you have committed adultery, or you know someone who has, there's a prayer of confession in the Bible, written by King David after he committed adultery with Bathsheba. It's preserved for us as Psalm 51: 'Loving and kind God, have mercy. Have pity on me and take away the awful stain of my sin. Wash me, cleanse me from this guilt. Let me be pure again, for I admit my shameful deed – it haunts me day and night. It is against you and you alone I sinned, and did this terrible thing. You saw it all and your sentence against me is just. . . . Don't keep looking at my sins – erase them from your sight. Create in me a new clean heart, filled with clean thoughts and right desires. . . . Restore to me again the joy of your salvation and make me willing to obey you. Then I will teach your ways to others.'

God answered David's prayer.

A notice hangs in every Registrar's office in the country. It reads: 'Marriage, according to the law of the country, is the union of one man with one woman, voluntarily entered into for life, to the exclusion of all others.' Adultery can happen because no marriage, of course, is perfect; all of us have a sense in our lives of an unfulfilled need of love, acceptance and intimacy. But God still wants our marriages to be satisfying.

Agatha Christie once remarked that 'an archaeologist is the best husband any woman can have; the older she gets, the more interested he is in her.' The bonds of matrimony aren't worth much unless the interest is kept up. So, how do we maintain the interest over the years? How do we stay faithful?

First, get a grip on your thought-life! The Great Wall of China was built over many hundreds of years to keep China's enemies from invading. It is so wide that chariots could ride across the top of it, and is one of the few man-made objects that astronauts can see from space. But the Great Wall did not keep the enemy out. All they had to do was bribe a gatekeeper. Despite the massive defences, there was an enemy on the inside that let the one on the outside in. So it is with our lives.

The gatekeeper of our hearts must be faithful, otherwise God's instructions will do us no good. You are the gatekeeper. Beware of what you let in! Even if you haven't committed adultery, Jesus has a message for us all: 'You have heard that it was said, do not commit adultery. But I tell you that anyone who looks at a woman lustfully has already committed adultery with her in his heart. If your right eye causes you to sin, gouge it out and throw it away. It is better for you to lose one part of your body than for your whole body to be thrown into hell. And if your right hand causes you to sin, cut it off and throw it away. It is better for you to lose one part of your body than for your whole body to go into hell.' (Matthew 5:27–30).

Many of us (especially men) have sex on the brain, and it's the worst place to have it. How often do you take a second look? A man and his wife were in a department store and a stunning woman walked by. The man's eyes followed her. Without looking up from the item she was browsing, his wife asked, 'Was it worth it, for the trouble you're now in?' Adultery can begin to play itself out on the stage of the imagination long before it occurs in real life.

Jesus says, 'If your eye causes you to sin, gouge it out.' He doesn't mean literally – after all, you can still look through the other eye. What he's saying is, take drastic action. The problem is not actually in the eye but in the heart. Jesus demands that we deal decisively and severely by radical spiritual surgery.

So, rather than pluck out your eye, don't surf the Internet for pornography. Rather than cutting off your hand, cancel an adult channel on cable television. Watch your thoughts: they become words. Watch your words: they become actions. Watch your actions: they become habits. Watch your habits: they become character.

A mind that persistently schemes is a mind that needs cleansing. Jesus calls lust 'adultery in the heart'. If we don't confess and turn away from it, it will eventually consume our thoughts. And if we encourage it with sexually stimulating films, books, magazines or social settings, then fantasy will become reality.

Perhaps you could follow the practice of Job, who said: 'I made a covenant with my eyes not to look with lust upon a woman' (Job 31:1).

The second thing to do if you want to stay faithful is to avoid dangerous liaisons. Watch how and when you are alone with someone of the opposite sex. Watch how you touch them. Watch out for that long lunch, that after-work drink, the times when you stay late and work together on a project. A newspaper editor once ran a competition for the best answer to the question: 'Why is a newspaper like a good woman?' The winning answer was: 'A newspaper is like a good woman because every man ought to have one of his own, and not look at his neighbour's.'

Clip Two

Connie is having a flashback. She's back on the street in which she first ran into Paul. The wind is raging, her knee is grazed, and Paul has just invited her into his apartment. But in the split second in which last time, she hesitated and things turned out so badly, this time, she sees the taxi coming along the road and calls for it. It draws up, she gets in, and waves Paul goodbye. He stands at his door, smiling; his pile of books stacked up to his chin. Connie waves from the car, and smiles, as she turns her back on the 'moment'.

The third way to stay faithful is to try, at all times, to meet your partner's needs. The apostle Paul wrote about this very frankly in his first letter to the Corinthians: 'The husband should not deprive his wife of sexual intimacy, which is her right, nor should the wife deprive her husband. The wife gives authority over her body to her husband, and the husband also gives authority over his body to his wife' (1 Corinthians 7:3–4).

A happy marriage is not so much about how compatible you are, but how you deal with your incompatibility. We all have different needs, and some experts suggest these break down along gender lines: women in particular need affection, conversation, honesty, openness and integrity. They are looking for trust, responsibility and reliability. Men place sexual fulfilment higher up the list, as well as friendship and support. But, of course, all our needs vary according to who we are. The goal in marriage is not to think alike, but to think together; and the key to a good marriage is to understand that it's a union of two forgivers.

Lastly, to stay faithful, value your marriage. Prove your faithfulness to your spouse.

There was a minister who always hoped he'd become a principal of a Bible college. Eventually he did. But as he fulfilled his dream and vocation, Alzheimer's disease struck his wife. Her health degenerated to the point where he could not take care of her and stay on as principal of the college. The man decided to give up his position, even though his colleagues could not believe it. 'What are you doing?' they asked. 'She doesn't even know who you are.' The man replied, 'She might not know who I am, but I know who she is. She's the woman I made a promise to – until death do us part.'

A successful marriage requires falling in love many times with the same person. In a marriage it is important to treat all disasters as incidents and none of the incidents as disasters. As it says in the Book of Common Prayer, we accept our spouses 'to have and to hold from this day forward, for better, for worse, for richer, for poorer, in sickness and in health, to love and to cherish, till death us do part.'

For a good marriage, walk with the Master – 'But if we walk in the light as he is in the light, we have fellowship with one another' (1 John 1:7). And work on the marriage – as Paul commanded the Colossians, 'Whatever you do, work at it with all your heart'.

7

Is My Future Fixed?

MINORITY REPORT
Mark Stibbe

2002 DreamWorks Pictures

Director: Stephen Spielberg

Starring:
Tom Cruise
Colin Farrell
Samantha Morton
Max von Sydow

Classification: PG 13

Based on a short story by Philip Dick

Minority Report is one of Stephen Spielberg's more complex films. Like his controversial movie *A.I.* (Artificial Intelligence), *Minority Report* is a science fiction film that poses deep questions in a melancholy light.

Minority Report is a film based on a short story by the celebrated science fiction writer, Philip Dick, author of *Blade Runner*. It focuses on a police chief called John Anderton, played by Tom Cruise. Six years before the story of the movie begins, Anderton's son is kidnapped. His body is never discovered. The effects on Anderton are massive. On the negative side, his marriage disintegrates and his personality deteriorates – so much so that he needs to resort to a drug called Clarity in order to get by. Positively, Anderton joins a new and radical police unit known as Pre-Crime, a unit dedicated to preventing murders before they occur.

How, you might ask, do the Pre-Crime personnel know where and when a murder is to be committed? Within the Pre-Crime headquarters, in a room known as 'the Temple', three 'pre-cognitives' are kept wired up to a computer and heavily sedated. These three 'pre-cogs' have the ability to see visions of the future. They have the particularly unpleasant gift of being able to see images of murderers and their victims. These nightmarish images are transmitted from the brains of these three pre-cogs onto a big screen. They are then arranged into a meaningful and coherent picture by people like John Anderton, in the presence of two authorised witnesses. As the picture of the future act becomes clear, Anderton (or whoever) dispatches a Pre-Crime unit to the scene in order to prevent the murder from actually taking place.

The key to the success of Pre-Crime is accordingly the three pre-cogs. The three people in question, two men and a woman, are called Dashiel, Arthur and Agatha – presumably after three of the greatest writers of detective fiction (Dashiel Hammett, Arthur Conan Doyle and Agatha Christie). Six years prior to the opening of our story, these three pre-cogs were discovered by Police Director Burgess and Iris Hinaman and put into a cloverleaf shaped pod filled with water. It is they who harnessed their predictive powers to the murder squad of the Washington DC of the future. For six years Anderton has worked his way up the career ladder in the Pre-Crime unit, arresting future felons on the basis of the pre-cogs visions. These men and women have been arrested, have had 'haloes' clamped onto their heads, and then been placed in a deep storage facility. Here they are watched over by a sinister individual known as Gideon, who plays the organ; endlessly playing ancient melodies such as 'Jesus, Joy of Man's Desiring'.

The film begins in the year 2054 with a man from the Justice Department visiting the Pre-Crime unit. His name is Detective Ed Whitwer and he is played by Colin Farrell. Whitwer is investigating Pre-Crime, convinced that the pre-cogs – because they are human – cannot be totally infallible. In the following scene he meets John Anderton and his team and expresses his concerns.

Clip One

The four men are in the control room of the Pre-Crime unit, adjacent to the Temple where the pre-cogs are sleeping in their pod. One of the Pre-Crime officers is explaining what happens when the pre-cogs see a victim and a murderer in a vision.

FLETCHER: When the pre-cogs declare victim and a killer their names are embedded in a grain of wood. Since each piece is unique the shape and grain is unique, the shape and grain is impossible to forge.

WHITWER: I'm sure you all understand the legalistic drawback to Pre-Crime methodology.

GEOFF: Here we go again.

WHITWER: Look, I'm not with the ACL on this Geoff, but let's not kid ourselves we are arresting individuals who have broken the law.

FLETCHER: But they will. The commission of the crime itself is absolute metaphysics. The pre-cogs see the future and they are never wrong.

WHITWER: But it's not the future if you stop it. Isn't that a fundamental paradox?

In walks John Anderton.

ANDERTON: Yes it is. You are taking about predetermination, which happens all the time.

Anderton rolls a wooden ball along a curved surface and Whitwer catches it just as it looks as if it is going to fall on the floor

ANDERTON: Why did you catch that?

WHITWER: Because it was going to fall.

ANDERTON: You're certain?

WHITWER: Yeah.

ANDERTON: But it didn't fall; you caught it. The fact that you prevented it from happening doesn't change the fact that it was going to happen.

WHITWER: Do you ever get any false positives? Someone who intends to kill their boss or their wife but they never go through with it? How do the pre-cogs tell the difference?

ANDERTON: Pre-cogs don't see what you intend to do, only what you will do.

WHITWER: Then why can't they see rapes, or assaults or suicides?

FLETCHER: Because of the nature of murder. There is nothing more destructive to the metaphysical fabric that binds us than the untimely murder of one human being by another.

WHITWER: Somehow I don't think that was Walt Whitman!

ANDERTON: No, it was Iris Hinaman. She developed pre-cogs, designed the system and pioneered the interface.

WHITWER: Speaking of interfacing I would love to say hello.

ANDERTON: To Hinaman?

WHITWER: (pointing to the pre-cogs) To them.

The camera pans round and looks through a large window at the three pre-cogs floating below in a pool.

The group walk through into the dimly lit room, led by Anderton.

WALLY: (a rather sick young man who looks after the pre-cogs) No, no, no.

ANDERTON: It's OK; this is Danny Whitwer; he's from Justice. Don't touch them (referring to the pre-cogs) or anything else. Just answer his questions and we will get the hell out of here.

WHITWER: Tell me how ...

WALLY: Shhh, they're sleeping.

WHITWER: (whispering) Sorry. Tell me how all this works.

WALLY: (explains scientifically, and then adds) We call the female Agatha, the twins are Arthur and Dash. In other words, we see what they see. They don't feel any pain. We keep their heads full of dopamine and endorphins, plus we maintain careful control of the serotonin levels. We don't want them to drift off into too deep a sleep. They can't be kept too awake either.

ANDERTON: It's better if you don't think of them as human.

WHITWER: No, they're much more than that. Science has stolen most of our miracles. In a way they give us hope of the existence of the divine. I find it interesting that some people have started to deify the pre-cogs.

ANDERTON: Pre-cogs are pattern recognition filters, that's all.

WHITWER: Yet you call this room the Temple.

ANDERTON: It's just a nickname.

WHITWER: The oracle is where the power is anyway, the power has always been with the priests even if they had to invent the oracle.

ANDERTON: (looking at the other officers) You guys are nodding as if you know what the hell he's talking about.

JED: Well, come on chief, the way we work – changing destiny and all that – we're more like clergy than cops.

ANDERTON: Jed, go to work, all of you.

WHITWER: Sorry. Old habits. I spent three years at Fuller Seminary before I became a cop. My father was very proud.

ANDERTON: What does he think of your chosen line of work?

WHITWER: I don't know. He was shot and killed when I was fifteen on the steps of our church. I know what it's like to lose someone close to you. Of course, noth-

> of my own so I can only imagine what that must have been like. To lose your son in such a public place like that. At least now you and I have the chance to make sure that kind of thing doesn't happen to anyone …
> ANDERTON: Why don't you cut the cute acting and tell me exactly what it is you're looking for?
> WHITWER: Flaws.
> ANDERTON: There hasn't been a murder in six years. There is nothing wrong with this system; it is perfect.
> WHITWER: Perfect, I agree. But there's a flaw. It's human, it always is.

It is interesting to note here how spiritual, theological and even Christian the discussion is in this scene. The room where the pre-cogs are kept is called 'the Temple'. There are three pre-cogs, a kind of Trinity. One of them is called 'Agatha', which in Greek means 'good'. The police officers regard themselves as clergy. The visions of the pre-cogs are viewed as a metaphysical absolute – i.e. as something spiritually revealed and completely incontrovertible. The future is regarded as predetermined, yet at the same time human beings have a choice – an expression of the age-old theological issue of predestination and free will. Detective Whitwer, who is investigating Pre-Crime, spent time at a theological seminary (Fuller) and is at home with the question. Indeed, Whitwer argues that the pre-cogs have restored some kind of hope in the divine in an age when science has robbed ordinary people of the miraculous. Whitwer finds it interesting that the public are beginning to deify the pre-cogs and he also recognises the priestly nature of the Pre-Crime unit's work. So the language throughout this scene is deeply religious and even Christian. It is hard to imagine a more spiritually tuned and theologically complex discussion in modern cinema!

And the issues *are* complex! On the one hand Christianity has, over the centuries, championed the view that God is entirely sovereign and that everything in his universe is predetermined by him, including the choice human beings make whether or not to accept his Son Jesus Christ. This view, associated with John Calvin, is usually known as Calvinism or the Reformed view. On the other hand, Christianity has also, over the centuries, championed the view that all human beings have free will and that they are able to choose whether or not to follow Christ. This view associated with James Arminius is known as Arminianism. Arminians differ from Calvinists in this respect: Arminians see predestination as God's foreknowledge of the way each person will freely choose to accept or reject Jesus Christ. While Calvinists tend to see divine foreknowledge as God causing people to make certain decisions, Arminians see it as God simply knowing in advance the decisions humans freely make.

Which is correct? Theologians have never finally decided which of these two positions is true. Indeed, a new option has recently been introduced known as 'the open view'. This states the future is partly fixed and partly open, that there are many actualities that God has planned that will definitely happen, but that there are also an amazing number of potentialities which we choose and create, and to which God responds without compromising 'the big picture' of what is predetermined. Of course, all this is mind-bendingly complicated, and many feel dizzy just at the thought of such ideas. My own personal view lies somewhere between Calvinism and Arminianism. Indeed, I have every sympathy with the great nineteenth century preacher Charles Spurgeon who wrote:

> When a Calvinist says that all things happen according to the predestination of God, he speaks the truth, and I am willing to be called a Calvinist. But when an Arminian says that when a man sins, the sin is his own, and that if he continues in sin, and perishes, his eternal damnation will lie entirely at his own door, I believe that he speaks the truth, though I am not willing to be called an Arminian. The fact is, there is some truth in both these systems of theology.

Of course, all these questions become far more acute when it is your own future that is at stake. This is exactly what happens in *Minority Report*. At the beginning, Anderton and Whitwer conduct the discussion about predestination at a purely abstract level. All this changes when the pre-cogs have a vision of Anderton himself committing a murder. When the name of a man Anderton has never met is engraved on the victim's ball, and when Anderton's own name is engraved on the murderer's ball, Anderton's life is thrown into turmoil. How can he possibly be predestined to commit a murder? Since his son's death, his whole life has been committed to preventing, not causing, violent death.

Clip Two

The scene opens with the pre-cog Agatha moving her head out of the water. Then we see one of the brown wooden balls falling down the victim tube and the name Leo Crow written on it.

Anderton walks into the room.

ANDERTON: Jed, how come you are not out there with 'Father' Whitwer?

JED: We're in motion with something. From what I can see we've got a white male victim about 5'10 approx. 170. He takes a round and goes out the window.

ANDERTON: Red ball?

JED: No, brown ball, this one is premeditated.

ANDERTON: Amazing, someone within 200 miles actually dumb enough to still do that.

JED: The victim's name is Leo Crow. This is case number 1,109, time of occurrence, Friday, 1506 hours.

ANDERTON: Search for location of future victim Leo Crow case number 1,109, pre-visualized by the pre-cogs, recorded on Holosphere by Pre-Crime. My fellow witnesses for case 1,109 are Dr Catherine James and Chief of Justice Frank Poller. Good morning.

JAMES and POLLER: Good morning.

ANDERTON: Are the witnesses ready to preview and validate 1,109?

POLLER: Ready when you are John.
JAMES: Standing by.
JED: Oh I love this part. I've got no address, last known or otherwise, no tax returns for the last five years.
ANDERTON: Check NCI and see if he's got a record. We'll send a protection team as soon as we lock location. It looks like federal housing, concrete and glass egg crates.
JED: Ouch! There's about a thousand of those in the district.
ANDERTON: Fractured images coming in, number's 9... maybe it's 6. Female, senior, she is smoking a pipe. She's laughing. OK, now I'm inside a room, windowpanes, and two figures resolving in the room. Looks like we've got a third party wearing sunglasses just outside the window.

Camera pans in on the pre-cogs' vision depicted on a screen.

CROW: You are not going to kill me.
AGATHA: (speaking from within the Temple) Goodbye Crow.

Camera focuses on to one of the images being flashed up. We see an image of John Anderton with a gun. He says 'Goodbye, Crow' and fires the gun.

ANDERTON: (shocked) Wait! Wait!
JED: You say something, chief?
ANDERTON: No.

At this point a brown ball (signifying premeditated murder) rolls down the tube. Both Jed and Anderton go to collect it, but Anderton picks it up. Jed does not see the name on it.

> ANDERTON: We've got time on this one, Jed. You mind going and getting me a piece of that cake they're eating down there; I'm starving.
> JED: Sure, chief. I think I'll get one for myself while I'm at it.
> ANDERTON: Take your time.
> *Jed leaves.*
> *The camera focuses on the brown ball with the name John Anderton carved on it.*

This is one of the most dramatic scenes in the film. John Anderton is presented arranging the fragmented images of the pre-cogs. As the music becomes more and more dramatic, his arm movements begin increasingly to resemble those of an orchestral conductor. He points to an image of an elderly lady smoking a pipe and laughing, to a picture of numbers on an apartment door, to a man wearing sunglasses outside an apartment window.

Finally, as the music builds up to a crescendo, Anderton sees a horrifying image coming into focus. It is a picture of himself, with a revolver in his hand, aiming at a man in a macintosh. Anderton is seen saying the words, 'Goodbye Crow', and firing. Crow falls out of the window to his death.

This, then, is Anderton's future.

From this moment on, Anderton chooses to run for his life. In fact, running is one of the recurrent themes in the film. Anderton knows that the pre-cogs are never wrong. Their predictions are a metaphysical absolute. They have to happen. His whole life is built on this premise. He never stops to question whether flight will actually cause him to run *into* his destiny rather than away from it. Nor does he pause to ask whether his interpretation of the visions mean exactly what his reconstruction assumes: that his act is premeditated murder. The idea of 'self-fulfilling prophecy' never seems to cross his mind either. Instinct, based solely on his theological and philosophical worldview, takes over and he runs. He runs, in fact, to the garden house of Iris Hinaman, one of the co-founders of Pre-Crime. The following dialogue ensues:

Clip Three

ANDERTON: I'm not going to commit murder. I've never met the man I am supposed to kill.

HINAMAN: And yet a chain of events has started, a chain that will lead you to his murder.

ANDERTON: Not if I stay away from him.

HINAMAN: How can you avoid a man you have never met?

ANDERTON: So you won't help me?

HINAMAN: I can't help you, nobody can, the pre-cogs are never wrong – but occasionally they do disagree.

ANDERTON: What?

HINAMAN: Most of the time all three of the pre-cogs will see an event in the same way, but once in a while one of them will see things differently.

ANDERTON: Why didn't I know about this?

HINAMAN: Because these minority reports are destroyed the minute they occur.

ANDERTON: Why?

HINAMAN: Obviously for Pre-Crime to function there can't be any suggestion of fallibility. After all, who wants a justice system that instils doubt? It may be reasonable, but it's still doubt.

ANDERTON: Are you saying I've haloed innocent people?

HINAMAN: I'm saying that every so often those who have been accused of a Pre-Crime might just have an alternative future.

ANDERTON: Does Burgess know about this, about this minority report?

HINAMAN: I used to joke with Lamar that we were the mother and father of Pre-Crime. Well, in my experience, parents often see their children as they want them to and not as they are.

ANDERTON: Answer my question, does Lamar Burgess know about the minority report?

HINAMAN: Yes, of course he knew, but at the time we both felt that its existence was an insignificant variable.

ANDERTON: Insignificant to you maybe but what about those people that I put away with alternative futures. Oh my God, if the country knew there was a chance....

HINAMAN: The system would collapse.

ANDERTON: I believe in that system.

HINAMAN: Do you really?

ANDERTON: You want to bring it down.

> HINAMAN: You will bring it down, if you manage to kill your victim. Oh my, that will be the most spectacular public display of how Pre-Crime didn't work.
> ANDERTON: I'm not going to kill anybody.
> HINAMAN: Hold that thought.
> ANDERTON: Why should I trust you.
> HINAMAN: You shouldn't. You shouldn't trust anyone, certainly not the Attorney General who just wants it all for himself, not the young federal agent who wants your job, not even the old man who wants to hang on to what he had created. Don't trust anyone. Just find the minority report.
> ANDERTON: You said the minority report's destroyed.
> HINAMAN: The record is destroyed, but the original report still exists; I designed the system so that whenever a report occurred it would be stored in a safe place but not declared.
> ANDERTON: What safe place is that?
> HINAMAN: The safest place there is.
> ANDERTON: Where is it?
> HINAMAN: Inside the pre-cog who predicted it. All you have to do is download it, darling.

Anderton is here talking to Iris, the woman who knows more than anyone about Pre-Crime. Iris says that the chain of events leading to Crow's murder is inevitable. Her justification is that the pre-cogs are never wrong. She then pauses and adds the crucial qualifier, 'though sometimes they disagree'. At this point Anderton's curiosity is aroused. What does she mean by 'disagree'? Iris explains that the normal pattern is for the pre-cogs to be in perfect unity about a forthcoming murder, but that just occasionally one of the three may have a differing view. This dissenting voice is known as a 'minority report' while the view of the two who agree is accordingly regarded as the 'majority report'. This minority report is an alternate future seen by just one of the pre-cogs. It is not acknowledged publicly, else the system would be regarded as fallible. But privately Burgess and Hinaman have known about these reports but kept them safely filed in the minds of the pre-cog who saw this different version of events.

Anderton of course is incensed. First of all, this means that the system he has given his life and soul to is not absolutely foolproof. Secondly, it means that one of the pre-cogs may have had an alternate vision of his own future, a 'minority report', which in turn means that his own destiny may not be as inexorably fixed as he thought. These thoughts, simultaneously inspire hopelessness and hope. From now on Anderton commits himself to finding this report. He discovers it is stored in Agatha's mind. So he resolves to return to the Temple to kidnap her and then download her vision of his alternate future.

Before he can do that, however, he has to take drastic action. Everywhere in the Washington of 2054 there are retinal scanners. These scanners are used by the Pre-Crime unit to scan the eyes of every single person moving throughout the city. If Anderton is to return to the Temple, it cannot be with his current eyes because he will be immediately identified. So, in a truly grisly scene, he goes to a black market surgeon and has his old eyes removed and someone else's eyes put in instead. The message is of course clear at a metaphorical level. Anderton is seeing things with new eyes (and the theme of seeing, like the theme of running, is a powerful one throughout the movie). But at a practical level, Anderton's new eyes allow him to pass through the city undetected by the scanners, to return to the Temple, and to abduct Agatha. Together they go to a virtual reality marketplace where Anderton forces an old grass to download the images from Agatha's mind. But there is no minority report. There is no alternate future. And Agatha and Anderton find themselves drawn into the very destiny that the pre-cogs had foreseen.

Clip Four

So Anderton and Agatha enter the apartment visualised on the screen in the Temple at the start of the film. There is no one there but on the bed are a thousand photographs of children. Apparently we are in the apartment of a serial paedophile. To Anderton's utmost horror, he finds photos of his own son on the bed. He assumes that the man who lives here is the man who kidnapped and killed his own boy. He starts to weep with rage. Agatha starts to appeal to Anderton with the words, 'You can choose!' But Anderton's emotions are too strong. The man – Leo Crow – walks in. Anderton assaults him, punching and kicking him. The scene that follows is incredibly powerful:

Anderton pulls a gun on Leo Crow, in the room seen by the pre-cogs. Crowe stands at the window. The face of a man peers through.

> AGATHA: You can choose .... You can choose.
> *Anderton hesitates. The alarm goes off on his watch – set for the exact time he was meant to kill Leo Crow. Anderton starts to read Crow his rights.*
> ANDERTON: Do you understand these rights?
> CROW: You mean, you are not going to kill me?
> *Anderton lowers his gun.*
> ANDERTON: Do you understand these rights?
> CROW: You are not going to kill me?

Anderton's future was seemingly fixed yet he chooses not to commit premeditated murder. Of course, there is a twist here, and indeed further twists subsequent to this scene. But the point is, Anderton's predestined, premeditated murder – foreseen by the pre-cogs – has not actually occurred. Anderton, responding to Agatha's plaintive, 'You can choose', has exercised his God-given free will. He has decided not to commit an act of murder.

In the final analysis, all of us can choose. However predetermined our futures may seem to be, whether because God, our environment or our genes say so, none of this destroys the most fundamental right of every human being to exercise their free will and to choose right from wrong. This applies to the decisions that we make on a daily basis. We can, as someone has said:

> Choose to love – rather than hate
> Choose to smile – rather than frown
> Choose to build – rather than destroy
> Choose to persevere – rather than quit

Choose to praise – rather than gossip
Choose to heal – rather than wound
Choose to give – rather than grasp
Choose to act – rather than delay
Choose to forgive – rather than curse
Choose to pray – rather than despair

Above all, we can choose whether or not to love God and his Son or not. The offer to choose life rather than death is always open to us in this life. We are free to say yes or no. If we say yes, we choose blessing. If we say no, we choose the opposite. As God says in Deuteronomy 30:15–20:

> [15] 'Now listen! Today I am giving you a choice between prosperity and disaster, between life and death. [16] I have commanded you today to love the LORD your God and to keep his commands, laws, and regulations by walking in his ways. If you do this, you will live and become a great nation, and the LORD your God will bless you and the land you are about to enter and occupy. [17] But if your heart turns away and you refuse to listen, and if you are drawn away to serve and worship other gods, [18] then I warn you now that you will certainly be destroyed. You will not live a long, good life in the land you are crossing the Jordan to occupy.
>
> [19] 'Today I have given you the choice between life and death, between blessings and curses. I call on heaven and earth to witness the choice you make. Oh, that you would choose life, that you and your descendants might live! [20] Choose to love the LORD your God and to obey him and commit yourself to him, for he is your life.'

In the final analysis, Christianity offers us two things: forgiveness from the past and a hope for the future. The death of Jesus at Calvary gives us all the opportunity to stop running from our sinful past and it also prevents us from running headlong into an uncertain future. But God will never force himself on you or me. He will not make the choice for us. As Agatha keeps saying to Anderton, 'you can choose'.

So can you . . . .

So what future do you choose?

8

IT'S WHAT YOU ARE ON THE INSIDE

SHREK

J. John

> 2001,
> PDI/DreamWorks
>
> **Director: Andrew Adamson and Vicky Jenson**
>
> **Starring:**
> **Mike Myers**
> **Eddie Murphy**
> **Cameron Diaz**
> **John Lithgow**
>
> **Classification: U**

Shrek is directed by Andrew Adamson and Vicky Jenson, and is based on the children's book by William Steig. This is an astonishing, delightful computer animation, and it's no surprise that the film took five years to make.

At the very start, we are introduced to Lord Farquaad. He is a small man with a big head – an authority figure who ranks low on the scales of integrity and bravery. This contemptible Lord lives in Duluc, a sterile and manufactured 'reality'.

He has ordered all the 'misfit fairy-tale' creatures to leave his realm, and they have been forced to re-locate in a solitary swamp. The problem is, the swamp is home to a green ogre, who lives all alone in the middle of it.

He has made his home in the base of a large, broken tree. The tree is a symbol of Shrek himself: a giant with a broken heart. Shrek has isolated himself in his swamp. He has built layers around his heart, like those of an onion.

His frightening appearance has resulted in people judging and rejecting him without ever getting to know him. As a consequence, he doesn't want to get to know anyone else – especially all the creatures who have invaded his space. So, in an attempt to get rid of them and regain his solitude, Shrek agrees to go on a quest for Lord Farquaad, in return for the removal of his new, unwanted neighbours.

His mission is to rescue the lovely Princess Fiona from a castle guarded by a fire-breathing dragon, so that she can marry Farquaad, who can then become king. A loyal, talkative donkey accompanies Shrek. And donkeys, as it happens, are symbolic of humility, patience and burden bearers.

A story in the Bible's Old Testament also contains a donkey who finds he can speak, and who promptly rebukes the spiritual blindness of its master (Numbers 22:27–33). This is exactly what Shrek's donkey does – he speaks words of wisdom and words of rebuke. 'Friends forgive one another,' he tells Shrek. He's certainly no ass. . . .

In fact, the donkey doesn't judge by outward appearance, and he brings the best out of everyone, including the fire-breathing dragon. The love and friendship nurtured by the donkey are able, in the end, to set both Shrek and Princess Fiona free from the 'Kingdom of Self.' Shrek is released from his swamp of rejection and Princess Fiona is released from her stronghold of fear.

They ride off in an onion coach to live happily ever after. Only the proud, selfish Lord Farquaad remains unaffected.

The underlying themes in *Shrek* all question our traditional ideas of beauty. We have been brought up in a world dominated by beautiful pop stars, glamorous actresses and striking supermodels. In the eyes of our all-pervasive media, those who are beautiful seem to have it all. And as sad and superficial as this may sound, this view is actually fairly traditional.

Indeed, fairy tales present a similar theme: the beautiful princess, after initial obstacles, marries her Prince Charming in shining armour and they live happily ever after. Of course, these wonderful ideals appeal to us all; every man would like to be the hero, while most women have dreamed of becoming the beautiful princess.

Sometimes (even subconsciously) our perceptions of beauty are driven by how we imagine they could be in an ideal fairy-tale world. In order to help us question these deeply rooted ideas, *Shrek* wonderfully turns the idea of fairy-tale on its head. On the surface, the film has all the elements of the archetypal story: a beautiful princess, a fire-breathing dragon and a scary green ogre. It even opens with the classic storybook beginning.

However, things are not always as they seem. Lord Farquaad is not your typical villain – he's short, for a start. Princess Fiona is not a fairy-tale princess: besides turning into an ogre every night at sunset, she proves more than capable of rescuing herself; and, among other things, she burps, and she sings so piercingly that she causes a bluebird to explode. The dragon doesn't get slain, and turns out to be a 'good girl'. The ogre, in turn, becomes the 'knight in shining armour' and the object of the princess's affection.

The many parodies serve to prove the moral of the tale – that the beautiful story does not have to be conventional. In line with the rest of the film, at the end Shrek and Fiona are not transformed into a picture-perfect couple. Instead, they remain as they are. The point is, Shrek and Fiona are beautiful despite their appearance, and their story is a confirmation that happy endings do not rely on beautiful exteriors.

Clip One

The donkey and Shrek are sitting on a rocky outcrop in the middle of nowhere. There is a tumbledown house behind them. Shrek tells Donkey how eveyone judges him before they even meet him and get to know him. 'That's not quite true', points out Donkey. 'After all, I didn't judge you on appearances alone, did I?'

Donkey goes to make sure the princess is all right. He creeps into the house where she is meant to be resting, and looks around for her in the dark, feeling more and more frightened and calling out for her. Then he gets the fright of his life, as he finds himself face-to-face with an ugly girl – an ogre, in fact. 'You've eaten the Princess,' he shrieks. 'Don't worry Fiona!' he shouts at the ogre's tummy. 'Keep breathing! I'll get you out of there.'

'I am Fiona,' she replies, and as Donkey slowly realises that this is, indeed, Fiona, he tries to calm down, while she explains that every night, as the sun goes down, she

> changes into her ugly self. It always happens, without fail. And she won't ever take on 'love's true form' until she experiences true love's first kiss.

Throughout the film, both Shrek and Princess Fiona embark on a journey of self-acceptance, or – put another way in the film – 'becoming comfortable in the skin you're in.' We see very clearly that Shrek struggles with his appearance: 'People take one look at me and say, "Ahhh, look, big, stupid, ugly Ogre,"' he complains.

As a result of his feelings of rejection, Shrek has shut himself away, and decided to live a lonely, solitary existence. Similarly, her 'night time' form repulses Fiona. Despairingly, she cries to the donkey, 'I'm ugly, OK?' She describes herself as 'this horrible, ugly beast', but knows this isn't how it's meant to be: 'I'm a princess, and this is not how a princess is supposed to look,' she explains. 'Princess and ugly don't go together.' She doesn't believe that anybody could ever love her: 'Who could love a beast so hideous and ugly?'

What about us? We work hard to make things appear different to how they really are. Think about how much money we spend on the 'outside': we wash it, brush it, comb it, spray it, curl it, colour it, tan it.... We try to smooth its wrinkles, lift it, make it smaller, make it bigger – and still we don't like it.

Short people want to be taller, tall people want to be shorter and large people want to be smaller. Light skinned people try to get darker and dark skinned people feel they'd be better liked if they were lighter. Perfectionists, let's face it, are never perfectly happy.

However much we try to guard against it, we tend to shape ourselves in the image others have of us. It is not so much the example of theirs we imitate, as the reflection of ourselves in their eyes and the echo of ourselves in their words. We mould our faces to fit our masks. And all the time we're fussing over the external parts, while the internal parts are neglected.

As Shrek so wisely comments, 'sometimes things are more than they appear'. He describes ogres like onions – 'they have layers,' he says, and insists that 'there's more to ogres than people think'. The message, that we shouldn't judge people before we get to know them, is both timeless and true. If we judge a book by its cover, we are often proved to be wrong. There's much more to a person than mere surface appearance.

Even an ogre like Shrek, who freely withdraws from having any contact with other creatures, has a suppressed desire for companionship. Appearances are very deceitful.

It's a theme that is picked up by the Bible. 'Don't judge by appearance or height,' says the book of Samuel. 'The Lord doesn't make decisions the way you do. People judge by outward appearance, but the Lord looks at a person's heart and their thoughts and intentions' (1 Samuel 16:7).

In fact, the Bible says that all humans are made in the image of God. In an image-obsessed world, that's something to think about. The Bible wasn't talking about what God looks like, but how he is – a Creator God who loves others for who they are, and seeks their love in return.

God looks beyond our nose, which we think is too long, and our feet, which we think are too big. He looks beyond whether we think we are too tall or too short or too heavy or too thin. He looks inside the heart and sees what is there.

So, what *does* God look for in us? He searches for a heart that will accept his love. God is no respecter of persons. It doesn't make any difference what you look like. He wants a heart that is ready to receive his love, and reflect that love to others.

I remember walking down the corridor of a hospital, when I saw someone in a wheelchair. I couldn't tell if they were male or female, because their body was so twisted and bent. It turned out he was a boy, and he was in one of those motorised wheelchairs that can be controlled by the movement of just a finger or two.

This boy was motoring up and down the corridor, going faster than all the people walking along. He went to the end of the corridor, turned around and came back. As he raced along, I looked into his face and saw a great big smile and a look of exhilaration. It was clear that he'd just got the wheelchair, and all of this was the expression of joy in his newfound mobility. When I saw his face, I forgot about his body. I only saw the big smile, the sparkling eyes and a look of wonder.

I think God is like that. He doesn't see the imperfections, the scars and scrapes. He looks straight into the heart. Is there love inside of you that reflects the love of God so that others can see?

Jesus once said, 'Blessed are the pure in heart, for they will see God' (Matthew 5:8). When we think of the heart, we tend to think of our emotions. We say things like, 'I love you with all of my heart' or 'I have a broken heart'. Yet in the Bible, the word 'heart' refers to more: it refers to our emotions, our intellect and our will.

That is why Solomon urges us in the book of Proverbs (4:23) to 'above all else, guard your heart, for it is the well-spring of life'.

The heart is the control centre of our lives. According to Jesus, 'purity of heart' isn't about believing the right things. It isn't about going through the right motions. It's doing the right things with right motives.

St Augustine once wrote, 'Before God can deliver us from ourselves, we must undeceive ourselves.' We need unmixed motives, and transparent integrity.

Abraham Lincoln, when told that someone had called him 'two-faced,' said: 'If I were two-faced, would I be wearing this one?'

Purity of heart isn't just the absence of certain negative things in your life; it's positively the very presence of God in you. It begins with the shedding of pretence, which leads to an absolute inner awareness of who you really are. 'Pure' is translated from the Greek word katharos, from which we get 'catharsis'. It literally means 'to make pure by cleansing from dirt, filth or contamination'. In classical Greek, the word was most often used to describe metals that had been refined in the fire, until they were 'pure' – free from impurities. Jesus wants us to have a 'pure', 'clean,' 'unmasked' heart. A pure heart is a forgiven heart. It's a heart that has been cleansed by the purifying blood of Jesus Christ.

A pure heart is one that is in a relationship with God: that repents of sins and seeks inward purity. Purity of heart cleanses the eyes of the soul so that God becomes visible. When Jesus said, 'Blessed are the pure in heart,' he was pronouncing blessing on those who are pure at the very centre of their being, at the very source of their every activity, not those who appear pure on the surface. In fact, he berated the Pharisees for metaphorically washing the outside of their lives, while leaving the inside dirty.

Clip Two

Shrek and Donkey are standing outside a beautiful cathedral. Inside, Lord Farquaad and Princess Fiona are at the top of the aisle, as a packed congregation looks on. They are about to get married, and are preparing to say their vows.

Donkey urges Shrek to get inside and, at the right moment, object. He should tell her how he really feels, and stop the marriage.

So, just as Fiona is about to kiss the nasty Lord, Shrek bursts in. 'I object!' he shouts. He walks down the aisle, as the onlookers gasp. To Farquaad's consternation, he tells Fiona how he really feels. Outside, the sun is about to set. This is the moment of truth for Fiona. She walks to the window, and says that she's been waiting to tell Shrek the truth – to show him who she really is. The sun sinks below the horizon, and she transforms again into her 'ugly' self. 'That explains a lot,' says Shrek. While Lord Farquaad screams, calls his guards and commands that she be locked back in the tower.

At that moment, the dragon crashes through a huge stained-glass window, the guards wither in fright, and the dragon promptly swallows the evil Lord whole.

Shrek and Fiona look into each other's eyes. 'I love you,' he says. 'I love you,' she replies. They kiss – for Fiona, it is true love's first kiss, the kiss that she has waited for all her life, to transform her into 'love's true form'.

> In a huge explosion of light and stars, which is so fierce that all the windows smash with the force, she is lifted up and caught in a magical, beautiful cloud. Then she falls softly to the floor. 'Are you all right?' asks Shrek. 'Yes,' she replies. 'But I'm still ugly. I thought I would be beautiful.' Shrek looks at her lovingly. 'But you are beautiful,' he says. Cue the celebrations.

As Shrek progresses, we discover that the characters find acceptance. Shrek is accepted and befriended by Donkey, and Fiona grows fond of him. Slowly, he finds that he can accept himself and be content with who he is. It is in the penultimate wedding scene that Fiona reveals her true identity to Shrek. In the knowledge that Shrek still loves her as she is, she can then accept herself.

Fiona says, 'I don't understand, I'm supposed to be beautiful.' Shrek replies, 'But you are beautiful.' This acceptance is confirmed in the final words of the film: 'And they lived ugly ever after.' Not only are they content, but happy.

A 6-year-old boy with an ugly birthmark on the side of his face was once brought to one of Mother Teresa's orphanages. He appeared fearful, unloved and uncared for. He immediately went and sat in the corner and wouldn't talk to anybody.

Mother Teresa walked over and knelt down beside him in the corner and said, 'Well, what do we have here?' Then she embraced him in her arms and kissed him right on the birthmark on his face.

The other children started clapping because they knew that

if Mother Teresa kissed the birthmark, it was all right. It made it beautiful, just because Mother Teresa said it was.

That is what God has done. He has embraced us and kissed us, through the death of his Son Jesus on the Cross. It's another one of those topsy-turvy fairy tales – God became human, and not even a very handsome one at that (so the Bible says). The all-powerful king of the universe made himself weak, gave himself into human hands and died for us, so that we could be made beautiful in God's sight.

If you are experiencing loneliness and rejection, then know that God looks beyond all those things that people might consider ugly and unattractive. He looks at your heart. He looks for love. He looks for purity.

If you have those things, you're beautiful in God's sight. If you don't have them, God wants to take you in his arms, the same way Mother Teresa took the little boy in hers, and embrace you with love and acceptance.

Conclusion

One of the things we have tried to show in this book is that God speaks to us through human stories. These stories, visually enacted on the movie screen, transmit values. Sometimes the stories are written by Christian writers and have, at the very least, a Christian subtext. The movie version of *The Lord of the Rings* would be a good example of this. Even though its author did not want to write a Christian allegory, the pre-Christian universe of Middle Earth still has many echoes with what Jesus Christ lived and taught. This is because Tolkien knew that even the most pagan stories contained shards of grace in them. Other stories are written by writers or screenplay writers who would not claim to be Christians at all. Yet the fact that they are still created in the image of God means that something of God's light comes shining through their own creativity. As Tolkien himself wrote: 'We have come from God, and inevitably the myths woven by us, though they contain error, will also reflect a splintered fragment of the true light, the eternal truth that is with God.'

So we conclude with a story, a true story about three men (who Mark Stibbe's father knew personally), one of whom was to come to see that God really does speak through even pagan stories:

It is Saturday evening 19 September, 1931. C.S. Lewis, Professor of Medieval Literature at Oxford University, invites two guests to dinner – J.R.R Tolkien and Hugo Dyson – to his rooms at Magdalene College. The conversation flows as the three men, all devoted experts of English Literature, pass the time discussing the deep issues of life. After dinner, Lewis encourages both of his friends to join him on a walk through the beautiful grounds of Magdalene College. They stroll down Addison's Walk and they begin to discuss the subject of mythology.

J.R.R. Tolkien is the Rawlingson Professor of Anglo-Saxon and shares with Lewis a deep love of mythology, particularly Norse myths. C.S. Lewis is not a Christian, though he has ceased to be an atheist. In very recent times he has discovered that God really must exist. In the Trinity term of 1929 he had written: 'That which I had greatly feared has at last come upon me ... I gave in, and admitted that God was God and knelt and prayed: perhaps that night, the most dejected and reluctant convert in all England. ...'

Lewis now believes in the existence of God, but he doesn't yet believe that Jesus Christ is the Son of God. As the three friends walk together, Tolkien proposes that mythology may provide the answer for Lewis. For Lewis, myth is in reality the great problem. If Jesus is God's Son, then what about all the myths of dying and rising gods that had been believed before Jesus? Were they lies?

Tolkien's answer is an emphatic no! The myths that can be found in just about every culture before the time of Jesus have immense value. They contain truth in them. God-given truth!

Just then – as Lewis later recalls – there is a rush of wind that comes so suddenly on the still, warm evening – and sends so many leaves pattering down – that all three think it's raining. They hold their breath.

Tolkien presses in with Lewis. He explains that human beings are not ultimately liars. Our myths are not lies. Though we may pervert the truth through our sinfulness, we are all of us made in the image of God. All truth comes from him, and all our ultimate ideals come from him too.

Tolkien helps Lewis to understand that the myths of gods who die and rise again are not worthless lies but dreams put in the hearts of men and women by the one true God. In making myths, human beings – says Tolkien – are sub creators, storytellers who make imaginative worlds because they are made in the image of a Maker. He goes on to share that in Jesus – God's crucified and risen Son – the dreams of many ages become a reality. Or, as Lewis is later himself to put it, myth becomes fact!

Tolkien and Dyson (a committed Christian) continue to talk with Lewis, now, retiring to Lewis' rooms on Staircase III of New Building. Lewis has been convinced by Tolkien's views on mythology, and the conversation now turns from mythology to Christianity. Lewis' problem is, and I quote, 'how the life and death of Someone Else (whoever he was) two thousand years ago could help us here and now'.

What is the point of all this silly talk in the New Testament of Christ's sacrifice and of the blood of the Lamb?

Tolkien shows Lewis that the answer lies in what they have already been discussing. He shows how the myths of dying and rising gods were in fact God expressing his heart through the imagination of human beings, using fictional characters. Now, in Jesus Christ, God has expressed his heart through a real person among real people. Now a real Dying God has entered human history.

Tolkien leaves at three o'clock in the morning. Dyson continues to talk with Lewis, walking the cloisters of New Building until four o'clock. He tells Lewis that the person who believes in Jesus Christ receives peace and forgiveness of sins. This is a real pardon from a real person.

Three days later, Lewis is sitting in the sidecar of his brother's motorbike on the way to a zoo. Lewis later writes, 'When we set out I did not believe that Jesus is the Son of God and when we reached the zoo I did.'

Nine days later, Lewis writes to a friend, 'I have just passed on from believing in God to definitely believing in Christ ... My long night talk with Dyson and Tolkien had a good deal to do with it.'

Describing his conversion in later years, Lewis is to compare his experience with an awakening: 'It was like when a man, still lying motionless in bed, becomes aware that he is now awake.'

On Christmas Day 1931 Lewis goes to church and receives Communion. By the middle of the following year – 1932 – he has written the first of countless books that are to make him the best loved Christian thinker of the twentieth century, *The Pilgrim's Regress*. He will go on to create his own mythological universe in the *Seven Chronicles of Narnia* – books which vie with Tolkien's *Lord of the Rings* trilogy for first spot in the best fantasy literature of all time.

Lewis is later to write what have become some of the most famous words ever written about Jesus: 'A man who was merely a man and said the sort of things Jesus said would not be a great moral teacher. He would be either a lunatic – on the level of a man who says he is a poached egg – or else he would be the devil of hell. You must make your choice. Either he was and is the Son of God: or else a madman or something worse. You can shut him up for a fool, you can spit at him and kill him as a demon; or you can fall at his feet and call him Lord and God. But let us not come with any patronising nonsense about his being a great moral teacher. He has not left that open to us. He did not intend to.'

So what is your decision about Jesus?
   Lunatic, Liar or Lord?

Mark Stibbe and J. John

The Life

J. John and Chris Walley

There is no denying the importance of Jesus Christ in the history of humankind.

He has walked through the last two thousand years of history, of empires, governments, political systems and philosophies and has remained as a dominant, challenging, yet mysterious presence.

In *The Life: A Portrait of Jesus* J. John and Chris Walley achieve an uncommon blend – a serious book for popular use and a popular book for serious reading.

If you want to know who Jesus is, then read *The Life* and be rewarded.

ISBN: 1-86024-283-9 ● Price: £8.99

Calling Out

J. John

Calling Out is a serious attempt to provide a practical, all-round guide, enabling all believers to share Jesus. Despite its wide-ranging scope, *Calling Out* is written for all Christians, from new believers onwards in a fresh, lively and jargon-free style.

A passionate and compelling guide to evangelism by one of its most gifted practitioners, covering the following areas:

- Why do we need to share our faith?
- What is the message we have to share?
- Why do most of us find it so hard to do?
- How do we answer all those hard questions?

ISBN: 1-86024-359-2 ● Price: £7.99

Calling Out
The Course
Leader's Guide

J. John

Calling Out is a practical, all-round guide that shows all believers how they can share their faith in a fresh, lively and jargon-free style. Now, this course will help to equip Christians to multiply their faith.

In *Calling Out*, J. John explained what he had learned about evangelism. This course – which follows the order of that book in seven sessions – is designed to help small groups work through some of the lessons that the Bible teaches about calling out effectively with the good news of Jesus Christ.

ISBN: 1-86024-232-4 ● Price £9.99

Calling Out
The Course
Participant's Guide

J. John

This *Participant's Guide* enables individuals to study the sessions in small groups and is ideal for churches peparing for evangelism.

Designed to be used alongside the *Leader's Guide*, the sessions are designed to enable participants to gain confidence in sharing their faith by studying the following important issues:
Why do we need to share our faith? ● What is the message we have to share? ● Why do most of us find it so hard to do? ● How do we answer all of those hard questions?

ISBN: 1-86024-446-7 ● Price £2.99

Coming soon ...

Prophetic Evangelism

Mark Stibbe

Mark Stibbe is fully committed to the view that it is not only biblical but also urgent to reinstate prophecy to its rightful place in evangelism. He argues that God wants to speak to believers about the lives of unbelievers, particularly through visions and dreams.

This book is really a user-friendly exploration of how prophetic evangelism happens in Scripture and in our experience today.

Prophetic Evangelism is not only a thoroughly biblical study on the subject but also contains many encouraging testimonies.